My Squad – Contact Information

	NAME	PHONE	E-MAIL
1			
2			
3			
4			
5			
6			
7			
8			
9			
10			

Unless otherwise indicated, Bible quotations
are taken from The New International Version
1984, of the Bible.

ISBN # 978-0-9845101-9-1

	The Squad Master Small Group Study
978-0-9845101-4-6	Guide
978-0-9845101-5-3	C2W Audiobook
978-0-9845101-6-0	Called to War2
978-0-9845101-7-7	Warrior Field Manual
978-0-9845101-8-4	Squad Leader Manual
978-0-9845101-9-1	Master Trainer Manual

CORE 300

TABLE OF CONTENTS

FOREWORD

Welcome to the Core 300! You have just embarked upon one of the most exciting, life changing adventures of your life. In this Squad Study Manual are oft hidden Biblical secrets to unlocking *a sustainable walk of victory in your life* as a Core Disciple of Jesus Christ.

The Warrior Course takes the new Recruit back to the time of 1300 B.C. where a young man, Gideon, was alone, hiding in his winepress, and sifting wheat. Because of seven consecutive years of intense oppression by the Midianite hordes, Gideon, like most adults of his time, felt incredibly disqualified for authentic service to God. God greets him at his farm by saying, "The LORD is with you, ***mighty warrior***" (Judges 6:12).

This greeting is for you and me. "Mighty Warrior."

We are at a time in human history like no other. In America, the church of Jesus Christ is on her heels. We are at war but have hunkered down to play feeble defense against the powers of humanism, culture, sensuality, and demonic attack. In Europe, the condition is much worse and represents a future shadow of what the church in America will become unless we act.

Many men in church today are disengaged, hiding in the grandstands and making small, if any, contributions towards advancing the Kingdom of God. However, the condition is much worse for men. Yet, like at no other time in history, Paul teaches us in 2 Corinthians 10, beginning in verse three;

> "For though we walk in the flesh, we do not war according to the flesh. [4] For the weapons of our warfare *are* not carnal but mighty in God for pulling down strongholds," (New King James Version)

And Jesus came to declare war on the kingdom of darkness and saw it as a key assignment from the Father...to usher in the powerful healing, deliverance and salvation of the Kingdom of God.

The rest is up to you. You can move through this teaching and discussion material as a classic "Bible Study" and gain little, or you can open your heart to the transforming power of God's Word and get out of the stands and into the Arena for God. This is the pace where we will learn to play offense in this war and take new ground personally and for those we love and care about. I pray that you choose to live in the Arena for the rest of your life on earth!

Art Hobba,
Founder, Core 300 Men's Ministries

So Others May Live (SOML)

"That day, 50 men came forward, six or seven men at a time. . . the feeling in the room was pregnant with purpose, yet electrified with anticipation.

Brothers in Arms watched as each new Warrior came forward to the conveyance line.

They were to be received by ordinary men, now leaders, who had joined the battle months earlier.

The recruits had all seen this beautiful Warrior Challenge Coin, engraved in brilliant gold and hand painted with each piece of Armor of God.

Now, it would be theirs.

That day, 50 men came forward, six or seven men at a time, table by table, led by their Squad Leader. As each squad came and stood in line, the other 130 men remained seated in honored silence, quietly praying for the recipients.

*As the weighty medallion was pressed into his hand by a traditional military handshake, the words of the Oath of Conveyance were spoken: **"Walk worthy,"** charged the leader . . . **"So others may live",** responded each new warrior. In the embrace that followed, moist eyes met one another as they moved through the line.*

They knew, as they walked back to join their Squad that night that their life would never be the same."

Introduction to Core 300: The Warrior
"Out of the Stands and Into the Arena"

Core 300 is a movement that calls Christian men as disciples…children of God who are committed to be Christ's emissaries and army on earth. We yearn to see the release of the Kingdom of God on earth for God's glory and mankind's benefit. His Word clearly has equipped us for victory in battle, and this battle takes place in the Arena of this present life.

Our Mission Statement:

> *"Boldly calling men out of the stands and into the arena, bonded in authentic community with other men, trained as warrior-disciples and servant leaders, to rescue those in need…all through the power and for the glory of Jesus Christ."*

Premise: We live in a fallen, foreign world. I John 5:19 teaches us that "We know that we are of God, and the whole world lies under the sway of the **wicked one**". (New King James Version)

What is this "Arena" God has called us to? Jesus' gives us a clue in his first recorded sermon after descending from forty days of fasting, prayer, temptation, and spiritual warfare with the Devil. In his first brief message, he underscores the nature of his Kingdom that was beginning its divine invasion upon this fallen planet.

> *"So He came to Nazareth, where He had been brought up. And as His custom was, He went into the synagogue on the Sabbath day, and stood up to read. And He was handed the book of the prophet Isaiah. And when He had opened the book, He found the place where it was written:*
> *"The Spirit of the LORD is upon me, because He has anointed Me*
> *To preach the gospel to the poor; He has sent me to heal the brokenhearted,*
> *To proclaim liberty to the captives, and recovery of sight to the blind,*
> *To set at liberty those who are oppressed; To proclaim the acceptable year of the LORD."*
> *Then He closed the book, and gave it back to the attendant and sat down. And the eyes of all who were in the synagogue were fixed on Him. And He began to say to them, 'Today this Scripture is fulfilled in your hearing'".*
> (Luke 4:16-21 New King James Version)

Jesus' first act of public ministry is to declare war on the evil forces of darkness, human suffering, and carnal bondage. Herein he defined the arena we are also called to. His defeat of the Adversary in the battle on the mountaintop of temptation is followed by this **formal declaration of war**. His mission is to announce the advent of the Kingdom of God and his ministry is focused to this end. He affirms his role in John 18:37:

> *"You are a king, then!" said Pilate. Jesus answered, "You are right in saying I am a king. In fact, for this reason I was born, and for this I came into the world, to testify to the truth. Everyone on the <u>side</u> of truth listens to me. "*

And in Matthew 10:34, Jesus states *"Do not suppose that I have come to bring peace to the earth. I did not come to bring peace, but a sword".* In fact the word "sword" occurs in scripture 448 times...almost as many times as the combined uses of "worship", "praise", and "glorify" (485).

Jesus asserts that the inevitable intersection of Christ's coming is conflict. A clash between Christ and the Antichrist, between light and darkness, between truth and lies, good and evil, sickness and health, and between bondage and freedom. He poured his life into twelve men, and a handful of women, who walked with him for three years. They established the first outposts of the Kingdom of his dear son and the mission of Christ is now reached the four corners of the world. Jesus is still calling us today to be His warriors and ambassadors to bring about the entry of his Kingdom into the world in which we live. The conflict between light and darkness rages on until he comes again, and the church has been endowed with all of the authority of the risen King of Kings! Yet as God's Warriors we cannot fight this battle alone. To fight against the forces of evil we must 1) **Work Together,** and 2) **Put on God's Full Armor of Protection** (Ephesians 6:11-18).

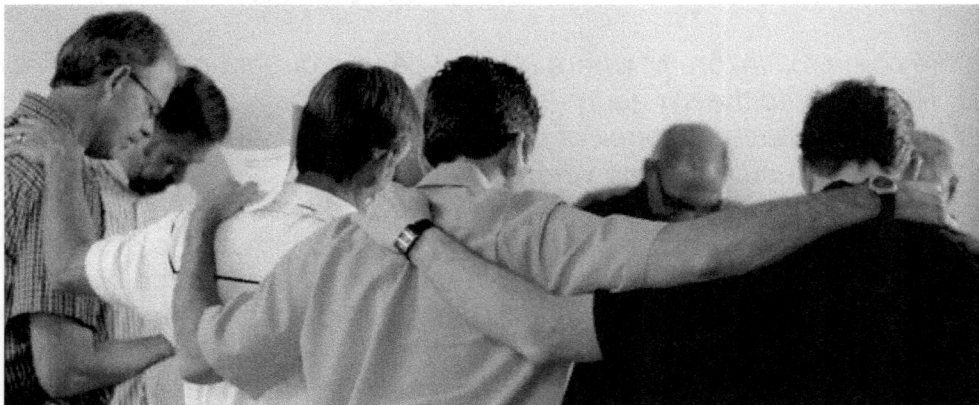

BOOT CAMP

As in any military service it all starts with basic training, so it is with God's army, whether you are a new recruit, or a seasoned veteran. The Core 300 movement involves Warrior training, and is designed to prepare you for battle to fight against the forces that have been arrayed against God for thousands of years. This Warrior Squad Study Manual is intended to help align you with the servant-leadership role you were created for and to establish you as a victorious disciple of Jesus Christ.

We begin with the first few sessions that break down the walls of self deception and isolation that we have built up over the past years. The second half of the training sessions is designed to build you up into a Mighty Warrior. Our meeting process follows this typical agenda:

WARRIORS WORSHIPING TOGETHER:

As our hero, Gideon, consistently responded to God with worship, we begin each session in worship.

> "God is the first priority of the church. Not people. Not ministry. Not growth. Not success. God and God alone occupies the place of ultimate and absolute priority in the church. Worship is about the priority of God in our affections. To worship God aright is to give Him our first, best love…In true worship, love is the supreme affection, and God is the exclusive object of our greatest love[1]"

We are called to *"Love the Lord your God with all your heart and with all your soul and with all your mind and with all your strength"* (Mark 12:30). Our response to that love is by declaring, out loud our deepest adoration and highest exaltation of who he is. This is the heart, action, and fountainhead of worship. It also serves as an *open invitation* and a *promise*. The Bible teaches us that God "enthroned upon the praises of Israel.[2] Praise is an invitation for him to come and be "enthroned" with us, his people. The promise is that *he will come* and be with us as our honored guest!

WARRIORS IN TRAINING - (PREPARING FOR BATTLE):

Each topic session will contain a key point outline to the weekly study, from which the students will fill in the blanks in their manuals, revealing the important content related to the truths about how God is calling us "Out of the Stands and Into the Arena".

---

[1] Bruce Leafblad, Professor of Music and Worship, Southwestern University Baptist Theological Seminary of Fort Worth, Texas
[2] Psalm 22:3

After each teaching, the Squad Leader will guide you through discussion questions that are designed to connect you, not only with Christ, but with one another, by calling each other to greater accountability and partnership so as to become more like Jesus.

SESSION 1:
INTRODUCTION TO GIDEON

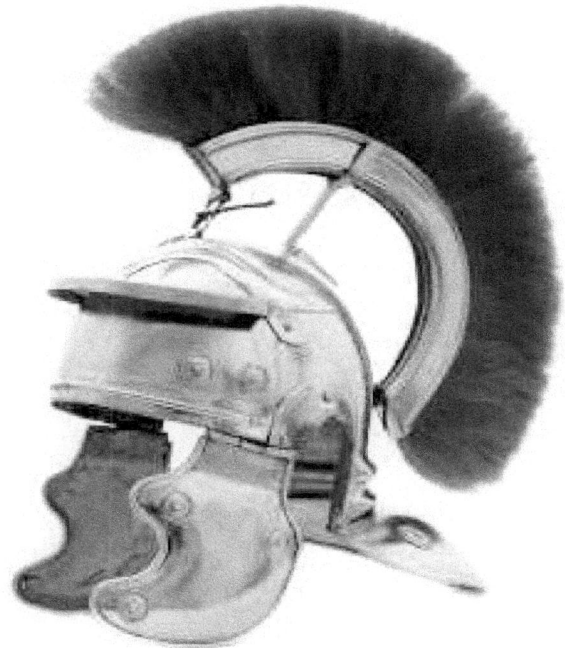

WELCOME!

OBJECTIVE

Objective

The objective of this session is to introduce you to the concept that we are at WAR and prepare us for the Warrior course.

OUR TALISMAN (THE CORE 300 COIN)

After the last session, we will gather together by Squad (table) and be presented with a beautiful Core 300 Armor of God coin. This treasured Talisman will be carried by each Warrior every day as a symbol of being alert and equipped in God's armor at all times.

SQUAD RULES

The military code of "No man left behind" is another part of the Core 300 culture. As we learn to be authentic with one another and walk through life together, sharing prayer needs and celebrating breakthroughs and victories, a bond will form that has a built-in code of commitment...to not allow your brother to be left behind in battle. We will grow to love each other and we, if taken down, will carry each other as well.

- Creating a _____ place

- Sticking to the same _____

- Looking for _____

- Table flow _____ everyone

- Committing to _____

- "What is said at the table, stays at the table."

GLADIATOR (SCENE XV)

The Battle of Carthage (Gladiator Clip): The film is loosely based on real events circa 2nd century BC. In the clip from the movie Gladiator, General Maximus Decimus Meridius, favorite of the Emperor Marcus Aurelius who is betrayed and murdered by his unhinged son, Commodus (Phoenix). Captured and enslaved along the outer fringes of the Roman Empire, Maximus rises through the ranks of the gladiatorial arena to avenge the murder of his family and his Emperor. The Gladiator scene demonstrates the power of "working" together.

WHY DID GLADIATORS LOCK SHIELDS?

- The unique thing that Maximus' leadership did with the Gladiators was to move the men side by side to lock shields for both _____ strength and defensive_____.

- The men outside the circle were _____ or wounded.

"Courage is resistance to fear, mastery of fear, not absence of fear. Except a creature be part coward, it is not a compliment to say it is brave."

WHY ARE MEN A STRATEGIC PRIORITY WITH GOD?

- ✓ If a father and mother both attend church regularly, _____% of the children will remain in their faith.

- ✓ If a father regularly attends church and the mother does not, _____% of their children's will remain in the church.

- ✓ When a father does not attend church, and the mother attends regularly, _____% of the children remain in church[3]

"To subjugate the enemy's army without doing battle is the highest of excellence."

- Sun Tzu, The Art of War

_____

[3] Source: Volume 2 of *Population Studies No. 31*, *The Demographic Characteristics of National Minorities in Certain European States*, published by the Council of Europe Directorate General III, Social Cohesion, Strasbourg, January 2000

WHAT ARE THE "STANDS?"

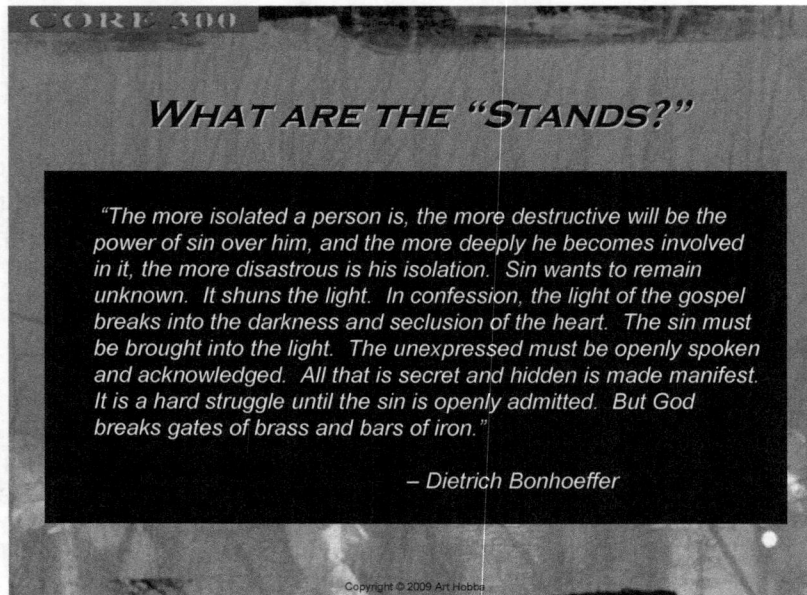

WHAT ARE THE "STANDS?"

"The more isolated a person is, the more destructive will be the power of sin over him, and the more deeply he becomes involved in it, the more disastrous is his isolation. Sin wants to remain unknown. It shuns the light. In confession, the light of the gospel breaks into the darkness and seclusion of the heart. The sin must be brought into the light. The unexpressed must be openly spoken and acknowledged. All that is secret and hidden is made manifest. It is a hard struggle until the sin is openly admitted. But God breaks gates of brass and bars of iron."

– Dietrich Bonhoeffer

Copyright © 2009 Art Hobba

WHAT IS THE "ARENA?"

What is this "Arena" God has called us to? Jesus' gives us a clue in his first recorded sermon after descending from forty days of fasting, prayer, temptation, and spiritual warfare with the Devil. In his first brief message, he underscores the nature of his Kingdom that was beginning its divine invasion upon this fallen planet.

Luke 4:16-31
"So He came to Nazareth, where He had been brought up. And as His custom was, He went into the synagogue on the Sabbath day, and stood up to read. And He was handed the book of the prophet Isaiah. And when He had opened the book, He found the place where it was written: "The Spirit of the LORD is upon me, because He has anointed Me to preach the gospel to the poor; He has sent me to heal the broken hearted, to proclaim liberty to the captives, and recovery of sight to the blind, to set at liberty those who are oppressed; To proclaim the acceptable year of the LORD." Then He closed the book, and gave it back to the attendant and sat down. And the eyes of all who were in the synagogue were fixed on Him. And He began to say to them, 'Today this Scripture is fulfilled in your hearing'". **(New King James Version)**

Hebrews 12:1
"Therefore, since we are surrounded by such a great cloud of witnesses, let us throw off everything that hinders and the sin that so easily entangles, and let us run with perseverance the race marked out for us."

YAHWEH: THE GOD OF WAR

- The LORD is a _____; the LORD is His name.

- One-third of the Bible was written in the context of _____ or _____.

Job 39:19-25
"Have you given the horse strength? Have you clothed his neck with thunder? Can you frighten him like a locust? His majestic snorting strikes terror. He rejoices in his strength; He gallops into the clash of arms. He mocks at fear, and is not afraid; nor does he turn back from the sword. The quiver rattles against him, the glittering spear and javelin. He devours the distance with fierceness and rage; nor does he come to a halt because the trumpet has sounded. At the blast of the trumpet he says, 'Aha!' He smells the battle from afar, the thunder of captains and shouting of war" ". (New King James Version)

WE ARE AT WAR!

1. Adam _____ in the garden. (Genesis 3:6-9

2. We've been playing defense and not _____.

3. Warfare makes us _____. (I Peter 5:8-10)

Be self-controlled and alert. Your enemy the devil prowls around like a roaring lion looking for someone to devour. Resist him, standing firm in the faith, because you know that your brothers throughout the world are undergoing the same kind of sufferings. And the God of all grace, who called you to his eternal glory in Christ, after you have suffered a little while, will himself restore you and **make you strong**, firm and steadfast.

I Am Gideon

Judges 6:1-10

Again the Israelites did evil in the eyes of the LORD, and for seven years he gave them into the hands of the Midianites. Because the power of Midian was so oppressive, the Israelites prepared shelters for themselves in mountain clefts, caves and strongholds. Whenever the Israelites planted their crops, the Midianites, Amalekites and other eastern peoples invaded the country. They camped on the land and ruined the crops all the way to Gaza and did not spare a living thing for Israel. . . they invaded the land to ravage it. Midian so impoverished the Israelites that they cried out to the LORD for help. When the Israelites cried to the LORD because of Midian, he sent them a prophet, who said, *"This is what the LORD, the God of Israel, says: I brought you up out of Egypt, out of the land of slavery. I snatched you from the power of Egypt and from the hand of all your oppressors. I drove them from before you and gave you their land. I said to you, 'I am the LORD your God; do not worship the gods of the Amorites, in whose land you live.' But you have not listened to me".*

Judges 6:11 - 12

The angel of the LORD came and sat down under the oak in Ophrah that belonged to Joash the Abiezrite, where his son Gideon was threshing wheat in a winepress to keep it from the Midianites. When the angel of the LORD appeared to Gideon, he said, "The LORD is with you, mighty warrior".

SCENE I: SOUTHERN ISRAEL (1100 B.C.)

- _____ = Abiezrite (Heb) "Father who helps".

    A village of Manasseh, SE Israel with the Jordan River as their eastern border; an agrarian and impoverished people with a survival mentality, they were fearful, hiding, and brokenhearted

- Seven years of _____.

- Cultural _____ of the Word of God.

    Judges 17:6 *"Every man did what was _____ in his own eyes."*

- **Religion** Polytheistic culture, superstitious.

    1) Baal was in charge of rain, fertility, crops, and livestock. Archeological

       diggings found under these 'High Places' were the place of regular

       _____ _____.

    2) Ashtoreth was Baal's "wife", their principal goddess. She was the
       personification of the reproductive principle in nature. Priestesses were
       temple prostitutes. Worship consisted in extravagant orgies;

    3) Yahweh was the God of Creation, Battle and Deliverance

CAST OF PLAYERS

Midianites were camel-riding nomads who attacked the Israelites when the harvest was ripe,
"like grasshoppers." You can think of them as an "organized mob." They were used by God to
discipline Israel.

- Midianites: Invaded the land to _____ it.

- Angel of the Lord: A _____.

- Gideon: (Hebrew) - "one who cuts down."

- Ba'al: In charge of the rain, fertility, crops, and livestock.

- **Asherah**: Ba'al's "wife" and their principal "goddess". She was the
  personification of the reproductive principle in nature. Priestesses were temple
  prostitutes. Worship consisted of extravagant orgies.

TABLE TALK

1. Why are men more "loners" than women?

2. Where do men usually "hide?"

A Citizen in a Republic

CITIZENSHIP IN A REPUBLIC
"The Man in the Arena"
Speech at the Sorbonne
Paris, France
April 23, 1910

By Theodore Roosevelt

"It is not the critic who counts; not the man who points out how the strong man stumbles, or where the doer of deeds could have done them better. The credit belongs to the man who is actually in the arena, whose face is marred by dust and sweat and blood; who strives valiantly; who errs, who comes short again and again, because there is no effort without error and shortcoming; but who does actually strive to do the deeds; who knows great enthusiasms, the great devotions; who spends himself in a worthy cause; who at the best knows in the end the triumph of high achievement, and who at the worst, if he fails, at least fails while daring greatly, so that his place shall never be with those cold and timid souls who neither know victory nor defeat.

Shame on the man of cultivated taste who permits refinement to develop into fastidiousness that unfits him for doing the rough work of a workaday world. "Among the free peoples who govern themselves there is but a small field of usefulness open for the men of cloistered life who shrink from contact with their fellows. Still less room is there for those who deride or slight what is done by those who actually bear the brunt of the day; nor yet for those others who always profess that they would like to take action, if only the conditions of life were not exactly what they actually are. The man who does nothing cuts the same sordid figure in the pages of history, whether he be a cynic, or fop, or voluptuary. There is little use for the being whose tepid soul knows nothing of great and generous emotion, of the high pride, the stern belief, the lofty enthusiasm, of the men who quell the storm and ride the thunder. Well for these men if they succeed; well also, though not so well, if they fail, given only that they have nobly ventured, and have put forth all their heart and strength. It is war-worn Hotspur, spent with hard fighting, he of the many errors and valiant end, over whose memory we love to linger, not over the memory of the young lord who 'but for the vile guns would have been a soldier'".

CORE CONDITIONING

- Read through Chapter 1 of "Called to War."

- Read Judges Chapter 6

- Email or call each of your Squad members and encourage them.

CORE 300

Traits of a CORE Disciple

Mission Statement

"Boldly calling men out of the stands and into the arena, bonded in authentic community with other men, trained as warrior-disciples and servant leaders, to rescue those in need...all through the power and for the glory of Jesus Christ."

Non-Negotiable Traits

- Regular study in God's Word
- Maintain a vital daily prayer life
- Available to increased levels of action and service for Christ
- Willingness to embrace Core mission statement
- Actively growing in spiritual leadership

Other Important Traits

- Commitment to and financially support your home church
- Serving the body or outreach in some capacity

Things Expected of the Core Men

- Do the "Core Conditioning"
- Participate in all Warrior Training Sessions (85%)

I am available and ready to serve as a Core Disciple as defined above.

_____   _____
       Print Name   Signature

I am not able now to join the Core Men but still want to be involved in Men's events

_____   _____
       Print Name   Signature
_____email _____phone

END OF SESSION

SESSION 1- PART II — ALONE, HIDING, AND DISQUALIFIED

In Session 1 we are going to dig in to the character and attributes of Gideon and his situation, as well as discuss the universal conditions of men. God, in his wisdom and foreknowledge, had decided to seek out a young man. God proclaims the good news that He is with him, and then, incredulously, calls him a "mighty warrior."

God does not make bad choices. He did not with Gideon, and He did not with you. We are often tempted to "pedastalize" Bible heroes. We far too often do the same with our pastors, priests, worship leaders, or elders. Historical men and women, especially those who participated in God's miraculous activities, are touchstones of inspiration for us. Too often, however, they become so highly revered that we unconsciously detach ourselves from the very real possibility that they are there to call us to similar, or even greater, actions of faith and sacrifice.

"Your playing small does not serve the world" – Marianne Williamson

THREE UNIVERSAL CONDITIONS OF MEN

1. Gideon was _____ in the winepress.

   - **Cynicism and Unbelief**: v13

   - **Pride**: Posturing, We have an image to maintain

   - **Competition**: Winning, Man Show, Extreme Sports

   - **Power**: Who is in charge here? . . .Certainly not you!

   - **Fear**: Being found out. Inadequate; Quiet desperation

To counter-act this first condition - Ecclesiastes 4:8-12

   - The power of _____, or jointly laboring together for a common goal (v 8-9)

   - The power to _____ another if he falls in the company of another man (v10)

   - The warm Hearth of _____ gained by being close to your brother (v11)

2. Gideon was _____ from the Midianites. (Genesis 3:8-10)

- When the wicked arise (Proverbs 28:12).

- We cannot hide from God (Psalms 139:7-8).

- Conscious sinning is _____ Atheism.

- Some shrink as an excuse for humility.

- Most of us _____ in our work.

TABLE TALK

1. Why do men hide?

2. What are YOU most prone to hide from?

THREE UNIVERSAL CONDITIONS OF MEN

3. Gideon felt _____ to serve God. (Judges 6:14-15)

The LORD turned to him and said, "Go in the strength you have and save Israel out of Midian's hand. Am I not sending you?"."But Lord," Gideon asked, "how can I save Israel? My clan is the weakest in Manasseh, and I am the least in my family."

Philippians 3:13, "forgetting those things which are behind . . ."
(New King James Version)

WHO'S YOUR DADDY?

a. We have bad _____. (Hebrews 4:15 –16)

b. "I will remember your sins no more." (Isaiah 43:24-25)

c. The _____.

William Manchester, author of **The Last Lion**, a biography of Sir Winston Churchill . . . *"Randolph actually disliked his son"*.

The father's harshness had hurt young Winston as a boy.

Churchill later wrote of his childhood:
"My father wouldn't listen to me or consider anything I said. There was no companionship with him possible and I tried so hard and so often. He was so self-centered no one else existed for him . . . he treated me as if I had been a fool; barked at me whenever I questioned him. I owe everything to my mother; to my father, nothing."

d. The Spirit of _____.

e. The Spirit of _____. (Romans 8:15 and Galatians 4:4-7)

NOTE: Though Sonship / Adoption becomes active at the experience of initial salvation it is often overlooked, untaught or incapable of being received "on earth" in real time, until a later stage in our lives. Sometimes it never occurs until after we die and go to glory.

f. God does not make bad _____.

TABLE TALK

1. How do you think the "wound" may have affected you. . . or may still be affecting you today?

2. What kinds of "Armor" do men wear? What about you?

CORE CONDITIONING

- Read Judges 6 again

- Pray for your Tablemates every day

- Read the text Introduction through Chapter 2

Optional Close: The beautiful and haunting poem below, often attributed to Nelson Mandela, was written by a woman, **Marianne Williamson**:

> Your playing small does not serve the world.
> There is nothing enlightened about shrinking
> so that other people won't feel insecure around you.
> **We were born to make manifest the glory of
> God within us.**
> And, as we let our own light shine,
> We unconsciously give
> other people permission to do the same.
> As we are liberated from our fear,
> our presence automatically liberates others.

Before you leave . . .

1. Please fill out the Core Traits form in your manual and hand it in to your Squad Leader.

2. Share any prayer requests at your table and pray for one another before you leave.

SESSION 2:
BLOOD ON THE FLOOR

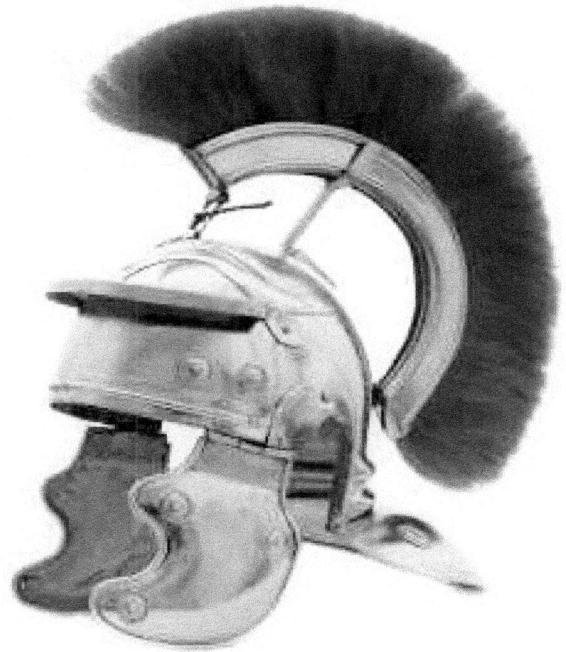

SESSION 2 — PART I: BLOOD ON THE FLOOR

Objective

The objective of this session is to understand Gideon more in-depth and the impact that this situation had on him.

Gideon's situation, like that of most men today, was complicated. Firstly, he wanted to provide for and protect his family. Secondly, he could not do that if he was not a good farmer-businessman. He had to make sure his assess (food, livestock, farmland, shelter, tools, and supplies) were producing what he needed and that they were protected from the Midianites.

TABLE TALK

"Without war, human beings stagnate in comfort and affluence and lose the capacity for great thoughts and feelings. They become cynical and subside into barbarism."

- Fyodor Dostoyevsky

-

1. Do you agree? Why or why not?

2. What other words for "war" could also make this truer?

GIDEON — THE WORSHIPPER

The dialogue between the Stranger and Gideon continues in Chapter 6. Gideon was facing the most awesome being to ever place foot on earth, the "angel of the Lord", and they were having a chat as if they were casual acquaintances!

Gideon did not realize that this was what many theologians believe to be a pre-incarnate visitation of the Son of God.

The LORD answered, "I will be with you, and you will strike down all the Midianites together." Gideon replied, "If now I have found favor in your eyes, give me a sign that it is really you talking to me. Please do not go away until I come back and bring my offering and set it before you." And the LORD said, "I will wait until you return."

Gideon went in, prepared a young goat, and from an ephah of flour he made bread without yeast. Putting the meat in a basket and its broth in a pot, he brought them out and offered them to him under the oak. The angel of God said to him, "Take the meat and the unleavened bread, place them on this rock, and pour out the broth." And Gideon did so. With the tip of the staff that was in his hand, the angel of the LORD touched the meat and the unleavened bread. Fire flared from the rock, consuming the meat and the bread. And the angel of the LORD disappeared. [22] When Gideon realized that it was the angel of the LORD, he exclaimed, "Ah, Sovereign LORD! I have seen the angel of the LORD face to face!"

Judges 6:16-22

GIDEON — THE WORSHIPPER

Let's talk about Gideon's Paradigm.

- First of _____ times he worshipped (before they actually engaged in battle).

- Gideon's Priorities were to protect his _____ from the Midianites =

  _____ mentality.

  o Why did he worship?

  o Where did he worship?

WHAT DID HE OFFER?

The Grain Offering: 1 Ephah

- Flour was used for _____

    o Ephah of flour-3/5 bushel 4.8 Gallons=72 lbs of bread (loaf=1 lb)
    o 2 loaves of bread per day to survive for a small family
    o Gideon sacrificed 36 days of food in the midst of economic crisis...

- Unleavened- without guile or _____

    o Gideon had no hidden agenda here.

The Meat offering: Young Goat

- _____ to the children and family

- Passover

- Potential

WHY BLOOD?

Sacrifice

- Loss through cutting.

- When were you last _____ _____ in your worship to God?

Matthew 19:29
"And everyone who has left houses or brothers or sisters or father or mother or wife or children or fields (job) for my sake will receive a hundred times as much and will inherit eternal life."

TABLE TALK

1. What do you do when faced with giving sacrificially? Discuss the obedience question.

2. What do you think you may have lost by not "anteing" up?

NOTES:

CORE CONDITIONING

- Read the textbook through Chapter 3

- Read I Samuel 13:5-13. What rationalization processes do you see in scripture between Saul and Samuel in the story?? Email and share any comments around to your squad during the week.

END OF SESSION

SESSION 2 – PART II: BLOOD OF THE FLOOR

In the second part of Session 2 we are going to discuss one of the cardinal cornerstones of defensive spiritual warfare and a foundation of protection (covering) that is missed by many believers who have rejected the concept of tithing as a starting point for giving.

THE OUTCOME

Jehovah Shalom - He saw God for the first time as the _____ ___ _____

- Peace as a _____ of sacrificial Worship

- Peace as a _____of the Kingdom of God

- Peace as a _____ of Victory ("peace = after victory = enemies his footstool)

Romans 14:17
"For the kingdom of God is not a matter of eating and drinking, but of righteousness, peace and joy in the Holy Spirit."

Hebrews 12:11
"No discipline seems pleasant at the time, but painful. Later on, however, it produces a harvest of righteousness and peace for those who have been trained by it."

FINAL THOUGHTS

- WHY? Because he _____.

- WHERE? It began at his _____.

- WHAT did he offer? Enough to really _____.

TABLE TALK

1. Why is it important to establish an "Altar" or Holy Place in your home?

2. Why do we have a difficult time, and often struggle giving enough to really hurt?

Core Conditioning: Setting Up Your Altar

- Read Judges 7 and the textbook Chapter 4

- Take a stone and establish an "Altar or Holy Place in your home

- Make an _____ to visit there with God every day in worship.

- Pray about how much you can give God as a sacrifice of worship that cuts deeply.

Pray this prayer to establish your 'altar:'

"Lord, I am here to meet with you. This shall be our special place . . . a place where I can come to worship, read your Word, and seek your face. This will be a place where I can get to know you better and even learn how to hear your gentle voice. Here is where I will regularly pray for those I love and care for. Here is where I will bring to you my deepest sorrows and where I will sit silently in times of confusion to find your peace. I consecrate this rock . . . and ask you to make it a holy place for you. Amen."

END OF SESSION

Session 3:
A Primer on Spiritual Warfare

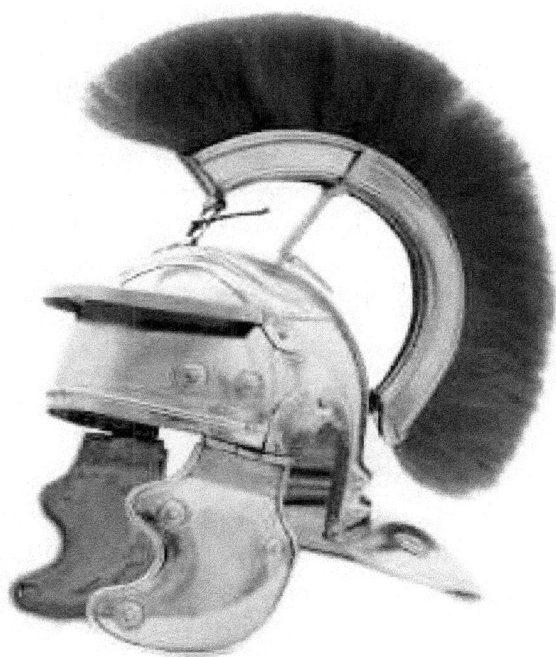

SESSION 3 – PART I: A PRIMER ON SPIRITUAL WARFARE

Objective

The objective of this session is to begin the preparation for spiritual warfare.

The salutation of "mighty warrior" is for you and me, not some historical hero. If you are going to become a warrior, you must first learn to fight. Consider the rest of the book and this course as "warrior training" textbooks.

In training camp, the soldier goes through rigorous conditioning, learning hardship and the art of war. Then he must apply himself to developing his skills in hand-to-hand combat, survival, weaponry, and the various tactics employed with those weapons. Moreover, he learns the critical value of the buddy system and building trust with his fellow soldiers in a small fighting unit called the Squad.

JESUS FANS IN THE STANDS . . .

- **Fantasy Warfare**
  At a Colts game there are lots of men with #18 Jersey …but there is only one Peyton Manning, and he is on the field.

- **Men love to root for their favorite teams**
  We even wear their uniforms and try to look fierce or like totally sold out fanatics! When they win…we feel as if we won…we feel the victory vicariously.

I Am Gideon!

- **But we did not really win at all**
  Only the men on the field experienced real victory. And even that real victory was men at play…not really men at war.

- **Men yearn to fight side by side with a band of brothers**
  Unfortunately, we have substituted spectator adrenaline flow at a sports game for engaging an enemy that even now is playing hardball…a ferocious lion on the offense to destroy your manhood, marriage and family.

Gideon — The Worshipper

That God was pleased with Gideon's offering is apparent in the way we see him walking with amazing favor and protection throughout his journey. When Gideon had brought the meat and the bread to the Lord, He told Gideon to take the meat and the bread, and place it on a rock. God then extended His staff and the tip touched the offering and from the rock itself flared an intense flame, totally consuming the offering placed upon the stone.

- First of _____ times he worshipped.

- He sacrificed 36 day ration of bread.

- He sacrificed the family pet and milk supply.

- God waited for him

- Fire consumed the sacrifice as it came up out of the rock

- We all received our prayer rocks to establish a holy place where we can meet with God every day.

THE THREE DIMENSIONS OF WAR

FLESH: James 1:12-15

Blessed is the man who perseveres under trial, because when he has stood the test, he will receive the crown of life that God has promised to those who love him. When tempted, no one should say, "God is tempting me." For God cannot be tempted by evil, nor does he tempt anyone; but each one is tempted when, by his own evil desire, he is dragged away and enticed. Then, after desire has conceived, it gives birth to sin; and sin, when it is full-grown, gives birth to death.

WORLD: 2 Corinthians 10:3-5

"For though we live in the world, we do not wage war as the world does. The weapons we fight with are not the weapons of the world. On the contrary, they have divine power to demolish strongholds. We demolish arguments and every pretension that sets itself up against the knowledge of God, and we take captive every thought to make it obedient to Christ."

DEVIL: Ephesians 6:11-13

"Put on the full armor of God so that you can take your stand against the devil's schemes. For our struggle is not against flesh and blood, but against the rulers, against the authorities, against the powers of this dark world and against the spiritual forces of evil in the heavenly realms. Therefore put on the full armor of God, so that when the day of evil comes, you may be able to stand your ground, and after you have done everything, to stand."

NOTES:

THE LAND = THE FLESH

James 1:12-15

"Blessed is the man who perseveres under trial, because when he has stood the test, he will receive the crown of life that God has promised to those who love him. When tempted, no one should say, 'God is tempting me.' For God cannot be tempted by evil, nor does he tempt anyone; but each one is tempted when, by his own evil desire, he is dragged away and enticed. Then, after desire has conceived, it gives birth to sin; and sin, when it is full-grown, gives birth to death."

Carnality of _____ _____ includes the seven deadly sins and represents the worst part

of humanity and depravity.

- Lust
- Envy
- Greed
- Wrath
- Gluttony
- Pride
- Laziness

As _____ was made from the soil of the earth, his flesh was cursed in the fall.

- **Diagnosis**: anger management' issues; sexual, substance other forms of self

  abuse; obesity due to caloric intake; binging, _____, lack of discipline;

  adrenaline/risk addict; excesses; fruitless - inconsistent life.

- **Treatment**: Open hearted _____ reading of the Word of God;

  _____ to authority, fasting, discipline, and

  _____.

THE SEA = THE WORLD SYSTEM

2 Corinthians 10:3-5

"For though we live in the world, we do not wage war as the world does. The weapons we fight with are not the weapons of the world. On the contrary, they have divine power to demolish strongholds. We demolish arguments and every pretension that sets itself up against the knowledge of God, and we take captive every thought to make it obedient to Christ."

- The World System is that system that _____ things, fame, wealth and power "more" highly than truth, God and other people. "More" of these things is this force's objective.
-

  - Materialism
  - Capitalism
  - Relativism
  - Humanism
  - Fascism
  - Racism
  - Narcissism
  - Hedonism
  - Communism
  - Atheism
  - Evolutionism

THE SEA = THE WORLD SYSTEM

- The Sea = the WORLD (cosmos-gk) _____

    (1 John 5:19-20; Matt 13:18-23; Rev 20:13-14; Eph 1:1-2)

- The World system is under the domain and _____ of Satan.

- The Thorns / Cares of this World _____ out our potential as men of God

    and render us fruitless.

- **Diagnosis**:
    Debt over toys or kingdom building:

    o _____ versus _____ of your

        resources

    o No or little spiritual _____

- **Prevention**:
    Choice of godly friends with godly values; social activities; serving less fortunate.

- **Treatment**:
    Breaking down the altars; _____ precious things away;
    contemplative prayer.

TABLE TALK

1. Think about the "Land," the "Sea" assaults, and;

   a. Pick *the* dimension where you are most often attacked.

   b. Share in your circle and discuss together.

2. *Listen.* Make suggestions on preventions and treatments and then pray for one another.

CORE CONDITIONING

- Contact your two or three closest friends and explain your desire to establish a "911" relationship, asking each of them to walk alongside of you and to pray for you daily.

- Share with your spouse, best friend or mentor the 1-2 areas you identified in your life where you are yearning for more freedom and ask them to pray with / for you.

END OF SESSION

Session 3 – Part II: A Primer on Spiritual Warfare

In the second part of Session 3 we will look at the enemy, his nature, attributes, and schemes.

The Bible teaches that eons ago the devil, or Satan, attempted to take over the throne of God in Heaven. He raised a following of one-third of the angelic host and together they were cast down from heaven by God.

Principalities = The Devil's Forces

Ephesians 6:11-13

"Put on the full armor of God so that you can take your stand against the devil's schemes. For our struggle is not against flesh and blood, but against the rulers, against the authorities, against the powers of this dark world and against the spiritual forces of evil in the heavenly realms.

"Given the same amount of intelligence, timidity will do a thousand times more damage in war than audacity."

Carl von Clausewitz 1780-1831

The Air = Satan

1. Demonic forces (PRINCIPALITIES) are arrayed against believers and can even control non-believers. Jesus taught that they seek to inhabit and express themselves through people.

- **The Air** = the regional and individually assigned/influencing _____ and

  principalities under Satan.

  (2 Corinthians 10:3-5; Eph 3:9-11; Col 2:14-16; Daniel 10:12-21)

- Demonized versus demon _____.

DEVIL FAQ'S

Let's take a moment and examine the nature of our adversary. We cannot hope for a victorious lifestyle without facing directly the truth of the one who desires the destruction of you and your family.

1. **His power over Christians has been broken.** Jesus/New Testament writers affirm that we have inherited the positional and earthly authority of Christ, in the church, through faith. This is both for the present and future. We are **now** seated with Christ in heavenly places with all powers in creation submitted under our feet.[2]

2. He is an old, patient, and **relentless schemer**. His plans take the long view and he will weave his web over the decades of our lives, chipping away at our resolve while he plans a great fall for every man and woman. But he is really interested in how he can leverage your weaknesses (or sometimes your strengths) to destroy you. Like an expert bowler, he will strike the head pin (you or me), which then is able to adversely impact those around you and even multiple future generations through the echo of sin in our lives.

3. He is the **original rebel against authority** and the source of the spirit of rebellion in al of society. *All* of what Satan has and does, and his kingdom, is fully corrupted. Hating God's designed authority, he seeks to corrupt those who have power and cultivates the lust of power in human hearts. His focal point is the church.

4. His **heart is filled with War**[4] *There will be no truce, no rest, and no reprieve in this war against the Saints until he is finally cast into the Lake of Fire .He actually thinks he can win, and as the end of these times approaches, his wrath will escalate[5].*

5. He is a liar and **the father of all lies**. Lies seek to breed his lying seed in us. First lies are exaggeration, self-defense, and rationalization. He seeks to train a child to avoid the truth regarding personal responsibility for their actions, then the child will be raised with the inability to perceive truth. Lying becomes the means of operation with others. The Father of

---

[4] Psalm 55:21(New Living Translation
[5] Revelation 12:12

6. He is **not omnipotent**. The Devil is a broken shadow of what he once was. The first great setback was when he was cast down to earth due to his rebellion against God. By jealousy, he wrought great destruction upon humanity with a reign over death, disease, and war. Then he was fooled into murdering Jesus. In Jesus' post crucifixion descent into Hell's domain, much of the enemy's power was broken with a wound inflicted by Christ. Many believe the Lord seized the "keys to death and Hades"[6] from Satan's hand at this time, redeeming mankind through his righteous sacrifice.

7. He is **not omnipresent**. As a singular created being, he must work strategically through the tactics of shoring up an evil World system. The balance of his forces is demonic entities assigned to key individuals and leaders, political arenas or strategic organizations.

8. He is **not omniscient.** Although he has the benefit of many thousands of years of *experience* of how we can predictably be manipulated, tempted, and intimidated.

9. He is the **author of Death**.[7] The apocryphal book of Wisdom, written a century before Jesus' birth, aptly says, "*…by the envy of the devil, death entered the world, and they who are in his possession, experience it.*"[9]

10. **He is a murderer** and the source of all thoughts and actions of hatred. Gangland violence, wars, sociopathic behavior, armed robberies, demonic possession, abortion, drunk driving, brawling, terrorism, physical abuse, sexual abuse, cancer, AIDS (and other deadly diseases) and suicides all have the spirit of murder it their core.

11. He is much **smarter than a fifth grader**…and thus you or me. As Eve discovered, it is dangerous to dialogue with him. Even the most powerful of angelic forces, the archangel Michael, when God assigned him to retrieve the body of Moses, did not affront him directly, but had to employ Gods direct authority by declaring "*the Lord rebuke you.*"[8] There is no place for glibness or testosterone-induced moxey when dealing with the enemy directly.

12. He **hates women** and has active plans to destroy their humanity[11], femininity, motherhood, beauty, glory and the female genders great influence for love, courage, wisdom and all that is good.

---

[6] Revelation 1:18; Matthew 16:19
[7] Wisdom 2:24 (The New American Bible, Oxford University Press – Apocrypha)
[8] Jude 1:9

13. He **hates children**. The passion of *his* fatherhood is to make disciples of Hell, and just as the great evils of the Khmer Rouge, Fascism, Nazism and Communism take the young and inoculate them with their poisonous doctrines, he knows that if he can bend them through their childhood years, they are likely to never learn to love their Creator and Savior.

14. He **hates men (and boys) most of all**. As we have discovered, he also knows that the linchpin of society…and of the growth and health of the church, is *men*.

15. We need to **understand his overarching strategy**. Like in the great game of chess, he seeks *to take out the Queen*. Like chess, the King (Jesus Christ) has empowered the Queen (the Church) as the ultimate power player on the chessboard of this earthly realm.

THE AIR = SATAN

- **Diagnosis**: #1 Obsessive and repetitive _____.

    o Spirit of _____.

    o Hatred / Murder / Unforgiveness

    o Rebellion

    o Spirit of _____. (fear of man = snare).

    o Lascivious Sprit = Bondages to Perversion

    o Addictions - substances

- **Prevention**: Do not give a _____ to the Devil (Ephesians 4:26-28)

- **Treatment**:

1. Confession and Repentance

2. Fasting with Prayer

3. Laying on of hands for healing/deliverance to _____ the attachment of the spirit that has been identified, in the Name of Jesus.

TABLE TALK

1. What dimensions of war are active in:

   - A Divorce?

   - "Workaholism?"

   - The Quest for Fame?

   - Frequent Worrying?

   - Masturbation?

   - Wrath/Anger?

2. Think about the "Air" assaults in your life and share one area where you need more freedom.

3. Pray for one another before you dismiss and throughout the week.

CORE CONDITIONING

- Read Matthew 13 and meditate on the Parable of the Sower. Which of the fours soils do you see in your life?

- Follow-up with your "911" relationships, asking each of them to walk alongside of you and to pray for you daily…as you commit to do the same with/for them.

- Read Chapter 5 of the text "Called to War."

END OF SESSION

WARNING: These next three to four weeks will be attended with significantly heightened attacks from the enemy (think about Normandy . . . we are dispossessing his land). The enemy is entrenched and will try to thwart these sessions with increased temptation, sickness, job and family emergencies, etc.

IMPORTANT: Make sure to be in vigilant prayer for one another . . . SOML!

Session 4: From Fearful Farmer to Baal Buster

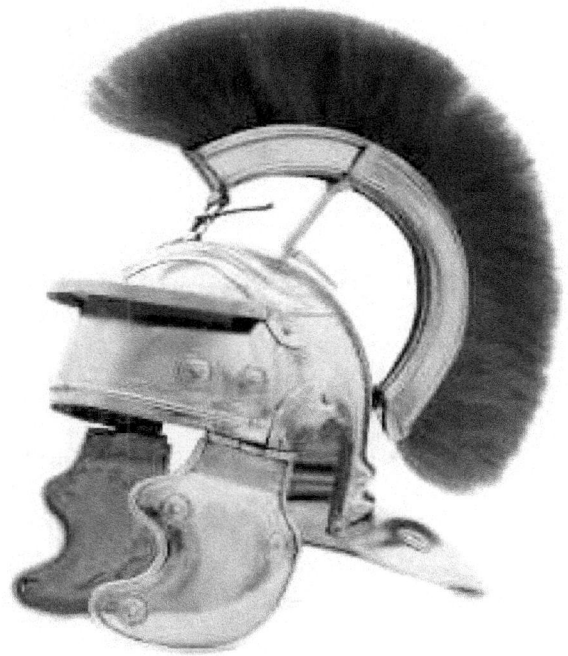

SESSION 4 – PART I: FROM FEARFUL FARMER TO BAAL BUSTER

Objective

The objective of this session is to identify and break areas of our lives where we compromise and even bow down to idols.

With the primer on warfare behind us, we can return to Judges 6. Gideon had passed his first test; by going against the grain of his own fears, overcoming low self-esteem and his own "common sense," and sacrificing deeply.

REVIEW

We live in a fallen, foreign world . . . "the whole world lies under the sway of the wicked one".

- The power work is in the Circle.

- Gideon was alone, hiding and feeling disqualified…like most men.

- God called him a Mighty Warrior nevertheless.

- Gideon worshipped four times before he ever fought a battle.

- Gideon gave until there was blood on the floor.

GIDEON'S GAME-FACE!

Judges 6:23 – 27

"But the LORD said to him, "Peace! Do not be afraid. You are not going to die. So Gideon built an altar to the LORD there and called it The LORD is Peace. To this day, it stands in Ophrah of the Abiezrites.

That same night the LORD said to him, "Take the second bull from your father's herd, the one seven years old. _____ your father's altar to Baal and cut down the Asherah pole beside it. Then build a _____ altar to the LORD your God on the top of this height. Using the wood of the Asherah pole that you cut down, offer the second bull as a burnt offering."

So Gideon took ten of his servants and did as the LORD told him. But because he was afraid of his family and the men of the town, he did it at night rather than in the daytime."

NOTES:

THE CONSECRATION OF GIDEON

- After worship is established Gideon is then given his first _____ – ____, to destroy his household and village idols of Baal and Ashtoreth. In this session we will look at Baal.

- The first test of _____ for Gideon was overcoming fear of man (his family and the local village).

- Was his _____ god (heritage of familial links)?

- He took the bull (Baal was symbolized by the bull).

  It had also been seven consecutive years that the Midianites had ravaged Israel, and the eighth occurrence was literally waiting on the horizon. This bull had survived seven years of hiding, nurturing and serving under Gideon's father's household.

- When compared to Gideon's young goat, the bull was _____.

  Priceless as the chief burden-bearer of this farming society; precious as a symbol of the strength of an ox in its prime and with an expected lifespan of 20 years; precious for its ability to procreate many times over in the years ahead. God, observing Gideon's sacrifice the day before had significantly raised the "ante" and the risk, far beyond that of taking from his own household assets. His father was the chief priest of Baal and an elder in the community.

- The bull _____ to his father.

THE CONSECRATION OF GIDEON

BAAL= CORE: _____

Fruitfulness of the harvest and livestock due to sufficient rains and protection from pests or diseases.

- There are _____ references to the god Baal in the Old Testament.

- Oftentimes Baal was confused with _____.

In 1929, excavation began in **Ras Shamra** in northern Lebanon. The remains of a palace yielded a library on the Canaanite religion:

- Emphasis on war

- Sacred prostitution

- Sensuous love and social degradation

- More recent excavation contained remains of over _____ children

Baal worship developed into the Greek god _____, the God of Time.

THE CONSECRATION OF GIDEON

BAAL WORSHIP

As the Israelites settled into the land, they encountered the fertility cult of Baal. They were easily convinced that while Yahweh may be God of the desert and God of battles and God of power, but it was Baal who was in charge of the more mundane aspects of everyday life, such as rain, fertility, crops, and livestock. They began to worship BOTH.

Baal

Baal worship included ritual prostitution to symbolize the fruitful 'watering of the womb' of mother earth by the god. Bring back the 'Rider upon the Clouds' as he was called... or the god of the storm or rain.

The altar of Baal was in the image of a bull with the head and shoulders of a man. This evolved into a "humanized god" with a budding staff, rod and/or sickle for harvest.

BAAL= _____ (Owner or Lord)

The dominant, earlier God of Egypt, first symbolized by the _____.

Called . . .

- "Most High Prince/Master"

- "Conqueror of _____ "

- "Mightiest, Most High

- "Supreme, Powerful, Puissant Warrior"

- "Prince, Master of the Earth"

BAAL WORSHIP

1. BAAL-GAD: *"lord of good fortune"* – Joshua 11:17

The world system will always throw in our paths a promised shortcut that invariably turns into a detour, taking us out of our ordained running lane so we might get rich quickly.

CONTRAST . . .
"A faithful man will be richly blessed, but one eager to get rich will not go

_____." - Proverbs 28:20

2. BAAL-PEOR: *"lord of the opening"* – Deuteronomy 4:3

God of "the opening" of the Midianites. Like lawless pirates, they simply took advantage of any opportunity or "opening" that presented an advantage to them. The opening is offered to us in the church when we use manipulation to get someone to give more or volunteer because we do not allow the Holy Spirit to move on a congregation or a family member. Seizing/leveraging the opportune "opening" is also common in business. The prosperity gospel does this as well,

_____: "You must love the one and hate the other". Jesus

Matt 6:20-24 But store up for yourselves treasures in heaven, where moths and vermin do not destroy, and where thieves do not break in and steal. [21] For where your treasure is, there your heart will be also . . . "**No one can serve two masters. Either you will hate the one and love the other, or you will be devoted to the one and despise the other. You cannot serve both God and money (Mammon).**

CONTRAST . . .
With God's ownership and your _____ – seek first His Kingdom!

REVELATION 3:14-17

"These are the words of the Amen, the faithful and true witness, the ruler of God's creation. [15] I know your deeds, that you are neither cold nor hot. I wish you were either one or the other! [16] So, because you are lukewarm—neither hot nor cold—**I am about to spit you out of my mouth.** [17] You say, 'I am rich; I have acquired wealth and do not need a thing.' But you do not realize that you are wretched, pitiful, poor, blind and naked."

Mammon can be seen as the polluted (lukewarm) water substitute for His living Water. Historically lukewarm (standing/stagnant) water was deadly or made you sick. Jesus is here saying that "lukewarmness" is related to seeing yourself as rich/wealthy independent of God and the reality is a totally naked and impoverished soul repulsive to Christ.

QUESTION:
How many Christians fit in this category and worship not Yahweh but Baal Peor?

TABLE TALK

1. Is idolatry well and alive in your life?

2. List and discuss how the various Baal gods may still exist in the church and our lives today.

3. Discuss the verse below.

   "Where your treasure is, there is your heart also." - Luke 12:34

CORE CONDITIONING

1. If you have not already done so, Go to http://www.biblegateway.com/, surf around and save to favorites. Use this tool regularly to find Bible verses and to cross reference. You will need this swordsmanship skill I the near future if you do not already have it.

2. Go to Google and study the term "deployment" and then drill down into "military deployment." Then Google "military occupation" (like the USA did in Iraq)

3. Read the parable of the ten minas in Luke 19:13-26. If military deployment in battle is supposed to result in victory, and victory leads, logically, to "occupation" through martial law, what was the intent of Jesus when he left this parable with His Disciples soon before His departure? "'Put this money to work,' he said, 'until I come back.' " (NIV) may be a poor domestic translation. Read again how the parable ends with the slaying of the unfaithful. Does look like a business transaction only?? Does the authorized (KJV) of "Occupy until I come" (KJV) make more sense in light of this? What does this tell you Jesus was inferring with His expectation of us after He bestowed upon us all the treasure (minas) all authority, salvation, eternal life, healing, the gifts of the Holy Spirit? Take notes of your thoughts in your workbook and share them online or over the phone with a couple of guys in your group.

NOTES:

SESSION 4 – PART II: FROM FEARFUL FARMERS TO BAAL BUSTER

In the second part of Session 4 we will continue to look at the different "Baal's" that were a constant and compelling attraction for God's people then, and the important parallels on how proliferations of this deity are still active in our society today, and unfortunately, in the church.

BAAL WORSHIP

3. BAAL-BERITH: *"lord of the covenant or contracts"*

- They grew accustomed to worshipping Gideon's gold _____.

- They carried a small god in their pockets as a "good luck" charm.

    CONTRAST...
    "Do not be unequally YOKED with an unbeliever." 2 Cor. 6:14

4. BAAL-HAMON: *"lord of wealth"*

Parable of the Sower: The seed that was sown among the weeds initially sprouted with promise, but soon found the "cares (anxiety) of this world and the deceitfulness of riches" choking out all the fresh, vibrant life that had begun to grow. There was to be no fruit for this soil . . . and no lasting legacy.

- The wisdom of Agur, as recorded as a prayer in Proverbs 30:8-9

    "Give me neither poverty nor riches – lest I be full and deny You and say, 'Who is the LORD?' Or lest I be poor and steal, and profane the name of my God."

    CONTRAST...
    You cannot serve God and Mammon; "The eye of a needle"

5. BAAL-HAZOR: *"Baal's village"* - **2 Samuel 13:23 -** _____

- "Conventional wisdom" is defined as ideas or explanations that are generally accepted as true by the public or by experts in a field.

- "Group think" – reflects the popular, media-supported viewpoints of the world.

- Hilary Clinton said *"it takes a village"* at the Democratic Convention in 1996.

- Submit to _____ group-thinking.

6. BAAL-MEON: *"lord of the dwelling"*

- MAN generally looks at the dwelling as a house; a safe place; prestigious address; a domain.

- WOMAN looks at the dwelling as her home; an _____ of who she is.

7. BAAL-TAMAR: *"lord of the palm tree"*

- A place of safety, rest or salvation (oasis). It could also mean the god of vacation. (Judges 20:33)

- God of escape - where we use worldly escapes, pharmaceuticals, alcohol, parties, etc., to find some peace/rest.

- God's rest – *"Come to me, all you who are weary (exhausted) and burdened (toil from weights on your shoulders or from grief and sorrow), and I will give you rest."* (Matthew 11:28)

  CONTRAST . . .
  God's gift of Rest
  "In my Father's house are many dwelling places . . . I go to prepare a place for you."

8. BAAL-ZE'BUB: *"the producer of flies"*

- Controller of this pest (flies), which was so common in the East.

- _____ or keep safe the storage of their harvest and "stuff."

CONTRAST . . .
Treasures in Heaven; YOU are the salt of the earth.

I Kings 16:33-34
"And Ahab made a wooden image. Ahab did more to provoke the LORD God of Israel to anger than all the kings of Israel who were before him. In his days Hiel of Bethel built Jericho. He laid its foundation with Abiram his firstborn, and with his youngest son Segub he set up its gates, according to the word of the LORD, which He had spoken through Joshua the son of Nun."

NOTES:

TABLE TALK

Read Psalms 139:23-24 out loud

1. What do you yearn for? This defines your 'success.'

2. How do we sacrifice our children to materialism?

3. It is alright to be afraid of the repercussions of destroying Baal in your life?

4. List your Baal's that you have knelt to.

- _____

- _____

- _____

PRAYER OF CONSECRATION AND BREAKTHROUGH

My Lord Jesus. Thank you for claiming my victory when you rose from the dead and for the present power of your resurrection right now. Thank you that you are also a mighty burden-bearer able to help me pull down any stronghold that has gripped my life.

I confess to You my sin of allowing other gods to influence and control me. Forgive me Lord and open my eyes to see the freedom that You have for me as your Mighty Warrior.

I confess the following altars in my life:

1.

2.

3.

And I repent of serving them in any way. I forsake them and renounce their influence in my life forever!

Now, in Jesus' Name and in His power and authority over every high thing of darkness, and over the world spirit, I break down the altars by name *(begin intense clapping as you name the Baal's and as they fall down, stomping your feet, crushing them entirely)*.

I cast them down, far away from my mind. I tear down every philosophy, every argument, every bondage, and every influence that these have had in my life and through me in my family.

Lord Jesus, I establish a new altar to you in my heart . . . totally devoted to you. Heavenly Father, I come to You as a free man, no longer hindered by the false gods of this present world.

Thank you for setting me free! Amen.

CORE CONDITIONING

1. Re-read Judges 8 and Chapter 6 of "Called to War."

2. Read Proverbs Chapters 2-8 focusing on verses with the following words:
   - Wisdom (she)
   - Adulterous (she), Prostitute, Immoral woman
   - Fear of the Lord
   - Fool / Simple / Naïve

3. Meet and pray with your 911's and confess the Baal's you have renounced.

4. Read Textbook Chapter 6

END OF SESSION

IMPORTANT REMINDER: *Make sure to be in vigilant prayer for one another . . . SOML!*

SESSION 5: FROM ASHERAH TO ASHES

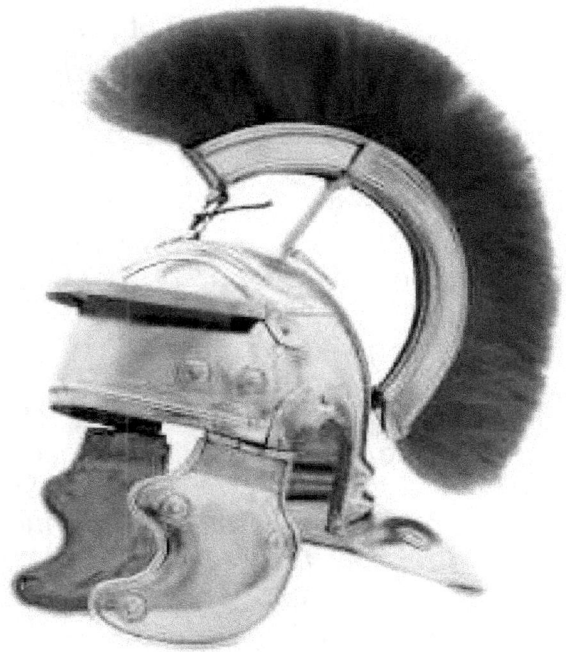

SESSION 5: FROM ASHERAH TO ASHES — PART I

Objective

The objective of this session is to a full Biblical swing at identifying and answering the questions about sex and how the forces of evil orchestrate warfare on your sexuality.

These next two sessions are critical. This teaching is the crux of why most men are in the stands . . . or fallen away from God. Many gave up as teens due to sexual failure . . . being overpowered by CWD (carnality, world system, devil).

Isaiah 6:1-8 *In the year that King Uzziah died, I saw the Lord seated on a throne, high and exalted, and the train of his robe filled the temple. Above him were seraphs, each with six wings: With two wings they covered their faces, with two they covered their feet, and with two they were flying. And they were calling to one another:*
"Holy, holy, holy is the LORD Almighty; the whole earth is full of his glory."

At the sound of their voices the doorposts and thresholds shook and the temple was filled with smoke. "Woe to me!" I cried. "I am ruined! For I am a man of unclean lips, and I live among a people of unclean lips, and my eyes have seen the King, the LORD Almighty." Then one of the seraphs flew to me with a live coal in his hand, which he had taken with tongs from the altar. With it he touched my mouth and said, "See, this has touched your lips; your guilt is taken away and your sin atoned for."

Then I heard the voice of the Lord saying, "Whom shall I send? And who will go for us?" And I said, "Here am I. Send me!"

GIDEON

Judges 6:24-27

That same night the LORD said to him, "Take the second bull from your father's herd, the one seven years old. <u>Tear down</u> *your father's altar* to Baal and cut down the Asherah pole beside it. Then build a <u>proper kind of altar</u> to the LORD your God on the top of *this* height. Using the wood of the Asherah pole that you cut down, offer the second bull as a burnt offering." So Gideon took ten of his servants and did as the LORD told him. But because he was afraid of his family and the men of the town, he did it at night rather than in the daytime.

ASHERAH

- What are the components and practices of Asherah worship as it relates to us?

- What is the big deal about sex? Why has Satan invested so much spiritual energy in sexual pollution, confusion, and compromise?

- How is your life, and that of many others, at stake in the war?

NOTES:

ASHERAH

o   Asherah appears _____ times in the Old Testament.

o   Means "Grove" - Canaanite _____ goddess-was often a carved pillar. Akin to "Mother Nature"

o   Also called Athirat; Wife of El, Mother of Baal and Ashtoreth (Aphrodite, Astarte, Ishtar).

o   Book of Jeremiah written 628 BC probably refers to Asherah when it uses the title "queen of heaven" in chapters 7 and 44.

o   1 Kings 18:19 - The four hundred prophets of Asherah, who eat at Jezebel's table.

o   Oftentimes erected next to Yahweh worship and forbidden by God of Israel. Once erected in the Temple in Jerusalem.

o   In Urgaritic texts, she is the consort of El, fertility Goddess and the wooden cult symbol that represents her. As El's first wife, she was said to have birthed 70 sons. All gods of the myths were born to Asherah and El, with the exception of Baal, whose parentage is uncertain. El had two wives but it was Asherah alone who nursed the newly born gods. Seeing as she had birthed so many children, it is only normal that she was worshipped as the true fertility Goddess, force of life and nature. She manifests in domestic herds and flocks, in groves of trees and in the nurturing waters. Her powers and her presence were invoked not only during planting time, but also during childbirth.

o   Asherah poles were places of fornication (with priestesses), orgies and goddess worship linked to Baal worship and the sacrifice of children.

o   Cutting down of Asherah was also the common word for "_____", "to sever completely," or "decapitate."

o   Gideon and his men chopped it into many smaller parts in order to use it for sacrificial firewood on the new altar of worship to Yahweh.

Asherah

1. Pornography (web or otherwise): You must violently _____the chains of habit and behaviors that fuel attraction.

2. _____ or adultery.
   Renounce and be freed from unhealthy behavior and relationships, past or present.

3. Harassing or lewd thoughts and images in the _____.
   Put on the helmet of salvation.

4. _____, lasciviousness, and perversions.
   Renounce and be freed from unhealthy behavior.

5. Objectification of others.
   Put on the helmet of salvation.

6. Homosexuality.
   Renounce and be freed from unhealthy thoughts and behavior.

7. Sexual abuse / _____.
   Inner healing, extending forgiveness, and purification.

8. Strip clubs, stalking, voyeurism.
   Renounce and be freed from unhealthy behavior.

9. Filthy _____, innuendo, leering.
   Renounce and be freed from unhealthy behavior.

ASHERAH

C.S. Lewis in The Great Divorce, Chapter 11

This except of the story brings us to a place where a man, who has died hours previously, is traveling on a very special bus with others who had suffered the same fate. The bus had made a travel stop where he is now having to make a decision as to whether he wants to enter heaven or not:

One of the passengers, an unsightly man, has decided to leave and is headed back to the bus. Sitting on his shoulder is a little red lizard, twitching its tail like a whip and whispering things in his ear. The man turns his head to the reptile and snarls,

> *"Shut up, I tell you!"*

> Just then, one of Heaven's radiant angels sees the man. *"Off so soon?"* he calls.

> *"Well, yes,"* says the man. *"I'd stay, you know, if it weren't for him,"* indicating the lizard. *"I told him he'd have to be quiet if he came. His kind of stuff won't do here. But he won't stop. So I'll just have to go home."*

> *"Would you like me to make him quiet?"* asks the angel.

> *"Of course I would"*, says the man.

> *"Then I will kill him,"* says the angel, stepping forward.

Then the man begins to panic at the thought of permanently losing the lizard, which he had, for years, grown accustomed to. There were the sweet fantasies, at times, that the creature whispered in his ear. But he is tired of carrying him around. He argues back and forth between the two beings, afraid to choose one path or the other.

The reasons for not killing the lizard are many (I have added some color commentary here from recalled personal conversations with my own "lizard").

1. He doesn't want to bother the spirit with killing it (God is too busy to worry about me and my problem).

2. It isn't presently bothering him because it went to sleep (I haven't felt much lust lately . . . maybe it is going away?)

He'll be able to get it under control himself through gradual process (no comment).

3. He doesn't feel well enough to go through with "the operation" (How will I be able to fill that hole in my soul without it?).

4. He thinks killing the lizard would kill him.

5. He'll go and get his doctor's opinion (back in hell), and come back later (let me study more and pray about this).

6. Then he asks why the spirit hasn't killed the lizard yet (If God wanted it gone He could take it away at any time…this must be my own personal "thorn in the flesh!").

The lizard has his innuendos and points to make as well (I have taken a few liberties here too):

1. The Angel can kill me but you will be killed in the explosion as well.

2. Every other guy has the same issues . . . it is only natural…like an Irish temper, right?

3. The lizard promises to behave himself in the future especially since you are so much smarter now that before.

Finally, in anguish, the man asks the Angel to kill the lizard, which he immediately reaches out and crushes. *"Ow! That's done for me,"* gasps the man, reeling back. He thought it was the end of him it hurt so much.

But then, gradually, something wonderful begins to happen. The man begins to be transfigured into a being of beauty and power . . . and much larger in size, yet still the same man. The joy of freedom fills his heart.

When he looks over to the carcass of his old wicked friend and companion, he sees that it also has begun to transform. Wonderfully it grows and changes into a mighty white horse, rippling with muscle, with a golden tail and mane. And he instinctively knew he was the new master of the magnificent beast.

Leaping confidently upon its bare back, they gallop away across the green plains, scaling majestic heights like a fiery comet, into the everlasting presence of eternity.

The secret, as so well revealed by Lewis' analogy, is that your very weakness, now mastered, will release a mighty multiplication of speed and strength to your walk with God.

WHAT IS THE BIG DEAL ABOUT SEX?

I Corinthians 6:12-20 (New King James Version)

All things are lawful for me, but all things are not helpful. All things are lawful for me, but I will not be brought under the power of any. Foods for the stomach and the stomach for foods, but God will destroy both it and them. Now the body is not for sexual immorality but for the Lord, and the Lord for the body. And God both raised up the Lord and will also raise us up by His power. <u>Do you not know that your bodies are members of Christ? Shall I then take the members of Christ and make them members of a harlot?</u> Certainly not! Or do you not know that he who is joined to a harlot is one body with her? For "the two," He says, "shall become one flesh," but he who is joined to the Lord is one spirit with Him. <u>Flee sexual immorality.</u> Every sin that a man does is outside the body, but <u>he who commits sexual immorality sins against his own body</u>. Or do you not know that your body is the temple of the Holy Spirit who is in you, whom you have from God, and you are not your own? For you were bought at a price; therefore glorify God in your body and in your spirit, which are God's.

Let's look at the side effects that we can experience:

1. As "living members" of one body, the church, it links our participation in Asherah's rites to those in the church. (1 Corinthians 6:12-20)

2. It causes a decline in our _____ for our wives, or even over time, to have children by them.

3. If you are single, there is a lessening of desire to _____.

4. Our general sense of _____ is increased not lessened.

5. It burns us. We feel immediately separated from our relationship with the Father. We find ourselves saying, "How could He want to be with me now?"

6. God is _____ of true open relationship with you for a while.

7. We are robbed of the strengthening love and joy of the Lord and the beauty of His holiness.

8. It subjects us, yet again, to the act of _____ and obeisance and increases the sense of hopelessness, disqualification, and isolation.

9. It compromises our ability and confidence to minister God's Word to those we love.

I Corinthians 6:8-10

"Instead, you yourselves cheat and do wrong, and you do this to your brothers. Do you not know that the wicked will not inherit the kingdom of God? Do not be deceived: Neither the sexually immoral nor idolaters nor adulterers nor male prostitutes nor homosexual offenders nor thieves nor the greedy nor drunkards nor slanderers nor swindlers will inherit the kingdom of God."

NOTES:

TABLE TALK

1. READ Ecclesiastes 4:9
   How is aloneness destructive to a man?

2. Where do your eyes go when you see a woman? Why?

3. Where does my sense of God go as I begin to engage in sexual thoughts or behaviors?

Think quietly for a few moments, about how much you have lost through sexual compromise in your mind and body. Write down a list of people who have been affected by your actions. Share one aspect at your table of how your life might have been different if you had walked consistently in sexual purity (not perfection) for your whole life.

- o Imagine what God could release of His power in you if you were totally free. Tell of one aspect that you believe would change in and through you towards others

STRATEGIC BATTLE SITES

- How is your life, and that of many others, at stake in the war?

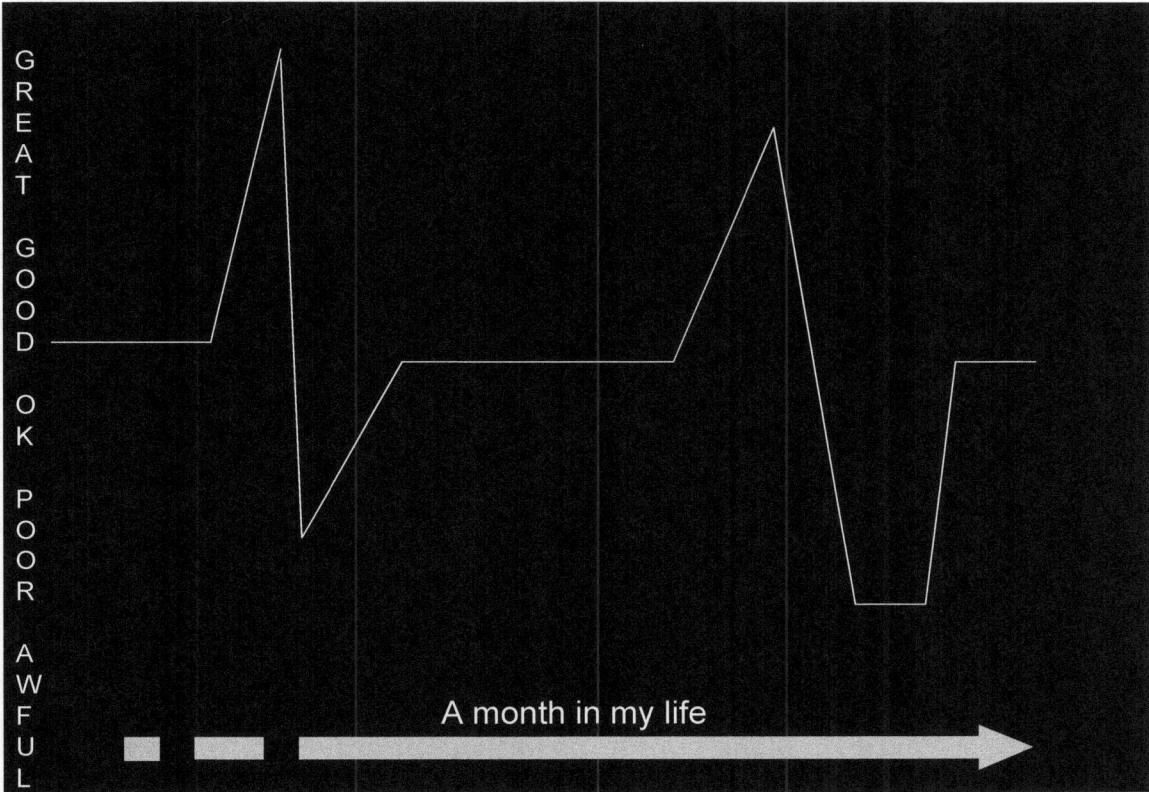

A month in my life

CORE CONDITIONING

- For your eyes only:
  Write an essay recalling the years of victory that have been sacrificed to Asherah in your life. What could life have looked like for you as a husband? A man? A Warrior? . . . if you had never bowed before her shrine in your heart.

- Review Chapter Six: From Asherah to Ashes, pages 136-144.

- Fast and Pray 24 hours before class

END OF SESSION

IMPORTANT REMINDER: Make sure to be in vigilant prayer for one another.

NEXT WEEK: Fast and Pray all day (drink water / fluids).

SESSION 5: FROM ASHERAH TO ASHES – PART II

The enemy has so seeded our world with the values and spirit of multitudes of Baal's and Asherah's that we often don't realize how he has set up our world to disable us. Our environment has been contrived to buffet our resolve, confuse our thinking and sap our strength. This is why we need to drink of His living water, daily . . . why we must ingest His Word and surround ourselves with the strength of trusted warriors who share the values of the Kingdom of Heaven.

ASHERAH

- How is your life, and that of many others, at stake in the war?

STRATEGIC BATTLE SITES

This diagram shows a typical guy who goes to church "flat-lining" in his spiritual life. No matter how men "posture," you can be assured that a vast majority of them share these feelings of spiritual delinquency as they beat against the feeble piers of faith.

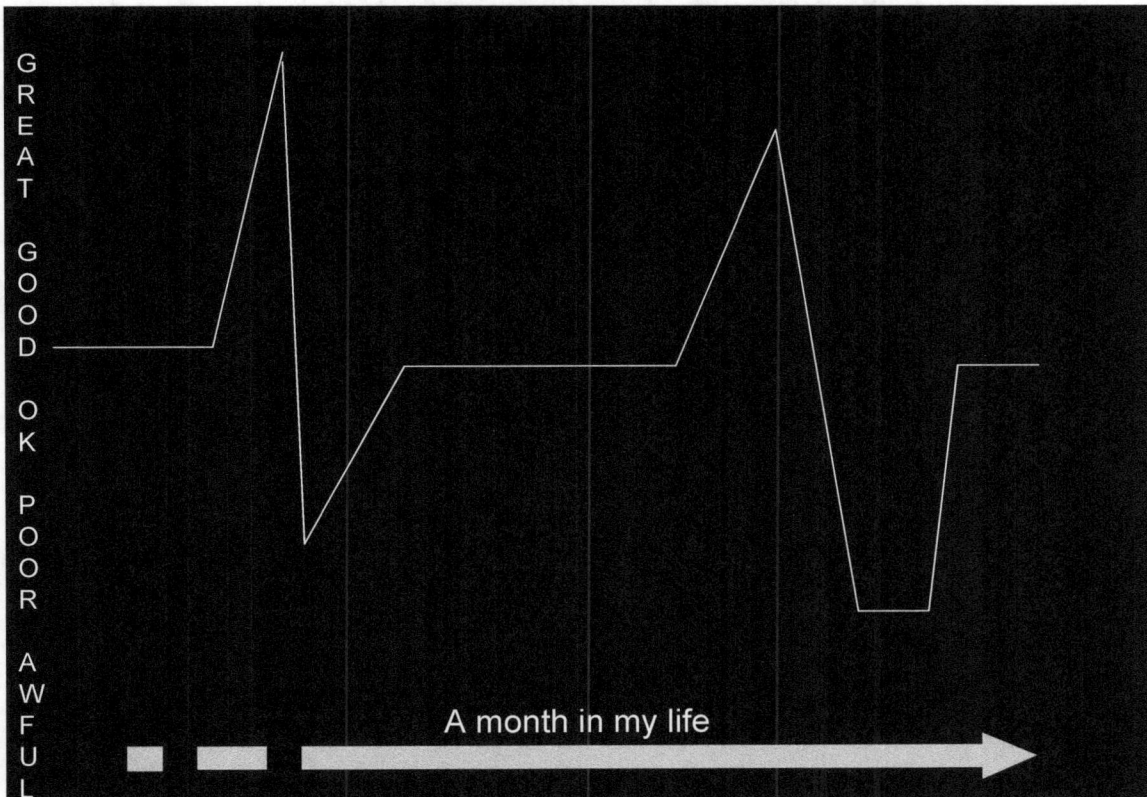

STRATEGIC BATTLE SITES

Let's take a more detailed look as this timeline.   Discontented, he goes to a men's retreat and comes back down the mountain inspired and pumped up. God may have lifted him so high he thought he'd never come down, or perhaps a sinful habit was broken when he confessed and prayed with a group of guys in his cabin.

However, the enemy tells you three things:

1. There was no real change.

2. Your freedom was only wishful thinking.

3. You are worse off than before . . . why ever hope again?

A big event happens in his life and he calls home and goes out to celebrate with his wife, has that "big feeling," and gets a little too carried away. That evening, they share a perfect meal together. He has too much to drink and is wired with adrenaline when they get home. He says goodnight to his wife and remains downstairs . . . ALONE, in front of the TV.

He has just spent an "unguarded" afternoon and evening growing more vulnerable by the rush of glory at work, the esteem of wife and kids, and a desire to buy more stuff. He is feeding his carnal nature.

Just like before, the way back is to Repent, Pray and Read the Word.

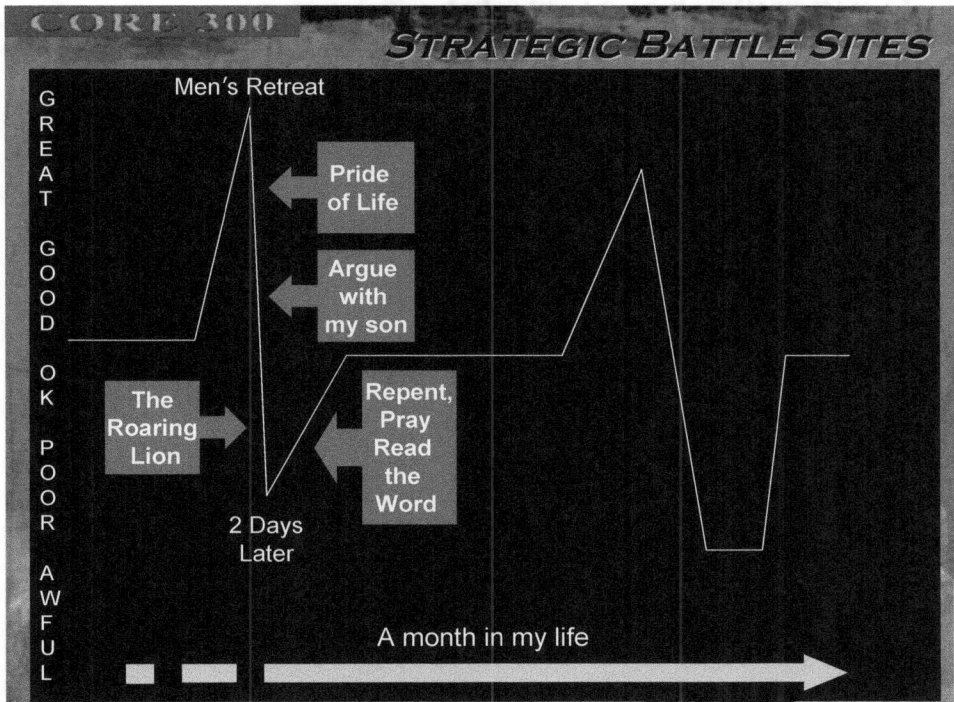

Strategic Battle Sites

GREAT GOOD OK POOR AWFUL

Men's Retreat
Pride of Life
Argue with my son
The Roaring Lion
Repent, Pray Read the Word
2 Days Later
A month in my life

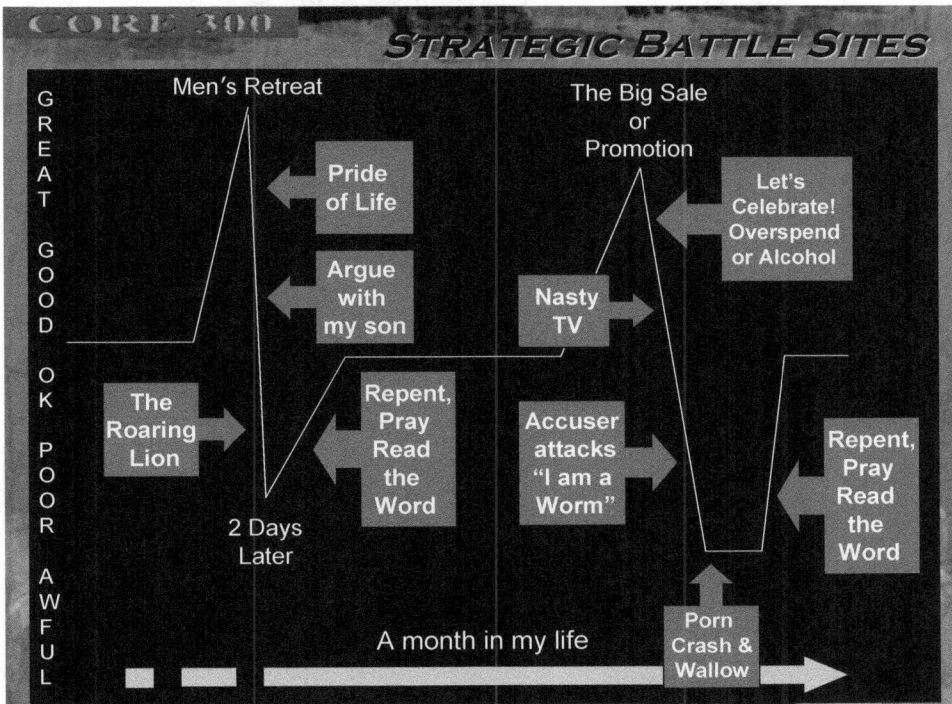

Strategic Battle Sites

GREAT GOOD OK POOR AWFUL

Men's Retreat
Pride of Life
Argue with my son
The Roaring Lion
Repent, Pray Read the Word
2 Days Later
The Big Sale or Promotion
Let's Celebrate! Overspend or Alcohol
Nasty TV
Accuser attacks "I am a Worm"
Repent, Pray Read the Word
Porn Crash & Wallow
A month in my life

HOW IS YOUR LIFE AT STAKE?

ZERA
In the Bible, the word "seed" is used 280 times. In Old Testament writings, there is a distinct focus on the "seed" of man, and success was often measured by the quantity of your sons and daughters and how large your tribe of grandchildren was. In other words, success was measured by your "personal fruitfulness."

SPERMA
In the New Testament, the most common word used for seed is the Greek word sperma. If God has put His seed (Word) in us, doesn't it make sense that this is where the enemy would strategically work to prevent us from speaking words . . . seeds of life?

Matthew 13:1-23

HOW IS YOUR LIFE AT STAKE?

1. Satan _____ that part of our body designed to pro-create new human life. It brings union symbolic of the Trinity and of Christ and His Bride.

2. Satan hates that part of our body that can _____ creative healing and be the mouthpiece of God.

3. Satan hates the words of life, light and truth that sets men and women _____ unto salvation.

4. For Millennia, Satan has attacked our sexuality to _____ our voice.

Proverbs 18:21
"Death and life are in the power of the _____.

TABLE TALK

1. What kind of tactics has the enemy used in your life to sideline you due to sexual compromise?

2. Look at all three arena's and discuss:
   - World System
   - Flesh
   - Demonic / Devil

3. Think about one area of your life that might have turned out different if you had remained pure, and share in your Squad.

BUILD A PROPER ALTAR

1. Sacrificed Priceless Bull

2. High place

3. Chopped down Asherah pole for fuel – (chopping is a violent act!)

4. _____ of the Holy Spirit

"The kingdom of heaven suffers _____ and violent ones are taking it by force" – Matthew 11:12

Get _____ at the Lizard of _____.

DESTROYING ASHERAH

1. Confess in unison to their own sexual failure . . .

2. Forsaking the goddess of Ashtoreth.

3. A cutting down (Gideon's name) of the altar.

4. Transformation / purification by _____ it with fire.

   o PRAY to be filled with the Word of God

   o WARNING: There is probably a vacuum in you where this stronghold resided and it is CRITICAL that you fill your mind and heart with Scripture all week long to replace the 'high place' that was once there. Read more of the Word of God this week than you have ever done before!

CORE CONDITIONING

- Hold your tablemates accountable to visit their rock and read their Bibles daily.

- Read Judges 7 and 8 (if you have not already) and Nehemiah 1 through 5.

- Contact your 911's and share the story of Asherah's being destroyed in your life. Commit to openness.
  DO NOT "WUSS" OUT IN THIS STEP!

- Warning…Be wary! Read 3 Chapters of Proverbs each day and Chapter 7 in "Called to War" this week.

END OF SESSION

IMPORTANT REMINDER: Make sure to be in vigilant prayer for one another.

NEXT WEEK: Be ready like Gideon, to be filled with the Holy Spirit and blow the horn of leadership!

SESSION 6:
BLOWING YOUR OWN
HORN

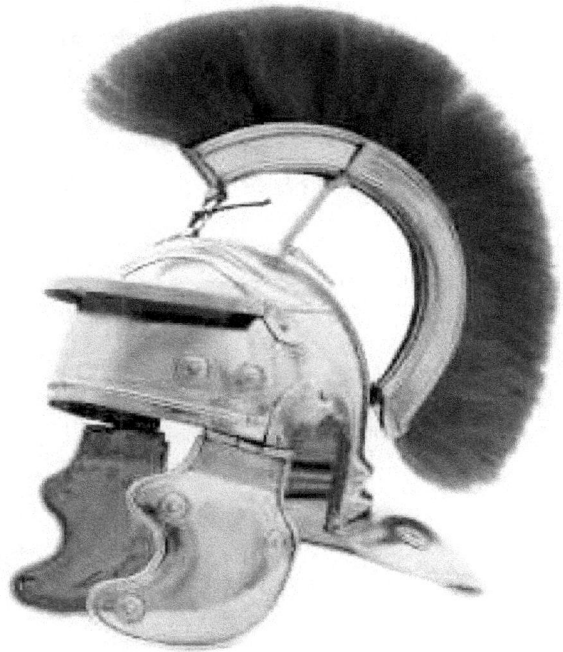

SESSION 6 – PART I: BLOWING YOUR OWN HORN

Objective

The objective of this session is to understand the call of leadership, and the values that are aligned with that leadership.

Gideon had succeeded in his obedience, his quest to destroy the worship of demons and restore the worship of Yahweh . . . but then things got deadly serious for everyone.

"Leadership is lifting a person's vision to higher sights, the raising of a person's performance to a higher standard, the building of a personality beyond its normal limitations."

-- Peter Drucker

STRATEGIC BATTLE SITES

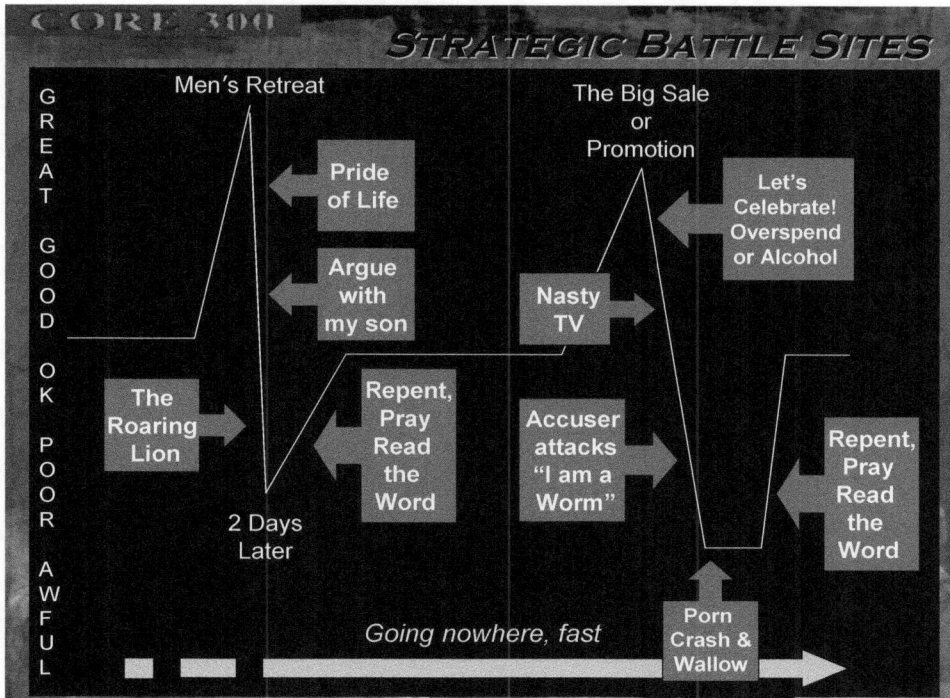

PAY IT FORWARD OFFERING: SEE LAST PAGE OF WARRIOR MANUAL

BLOWING YOUR OWN HORN

Judges 6:33-35
"Now all the Midianites, Amalekites and other eastern peoples joined forces and crossed over the Jordan and camped in the Valley of Jezreel. Then the Spirit of the LORD came upon Gideon, and he blew a trumpet, summoning the Abiezrites to follow him. He sent messengers throughout Manasseh, calling them to arms, and also into Asher, Zebulun and Naphtali, so that they too went up to meet them."

Four Virtues: Prudence, Temperance, Justice, and Fortitude

- Key Component of Leadership is Courage, which is the heart of Fortitude.

LEADERSHIP COURAGE

Illustration of Fortitude:
The miraculous victory of the English over the French at Agincourt came on Saint Crispin's Day in 1415, and falls on 25 October. It is the feast day of the Christian saints (twin brothers) Crispin and Crispians who were martyred in 286 BC. The following is from a pre-dawn oration from Henry V to his troops before the Battle of Agincourt.

> *"This story shall the good man teach his son;*
> *And Crispin Crispian shall ne'er go by,*
> *From this day to the ending of the world,*
> *But we in it shall be remember'd;*
> ***We few, we happy few, we band of brothers***
> *For he to-day that sheds his blood with me*
> *Shall be my brother; be he ne'er so vile,*
> *This day shall gentle his condition*
> *And gentlemen in England now a-bed*
> *Shall think themselves accursed they were not here,*
> *And hold their manhood's cheap whiles any speaks*
> *That fought with us upon Saint Crispin's day. "*

-- Henry V, William Shakespeare 1598 (emphasis mine);

BRAVERY VS. COURAGE

"Much Christian leadership is exercised by people who do not know how to develop healthy, intimate relationships and have opted for power and control instead."
- Henri Nouwen

1. Describe a hero in your life. (Note: You can't use Jesus for this).

2. Why do you admire them?

3. Were they Brave or Courageous?

LEADERSHIP COURAGE

Leadership failures often result when we put tasks and things in front of people. Even worse is when we allow our unique "flavor" of doctrine to divide us as believers. Looking down our noses at someone from a different tradition causes divisiveness between denominations.

> *"After fifteen years of diligent digging into the world around me, I have reached several conclusions about the future of the Christian church in America. The central conclusion is that the American church is dying due to a lack of strong leadership. In this time of unprecedented opportunity and plentiful resources, the church is actually losing influence. The primary reason is the lack of leadership. Nothing is more important than **LEADERSHIP**."*

Christian Schwarz, in his book *"Natural Church Development*

LEADERSHIP PRE-REQUISITE

Your _____ determine your behavior.

Values Definition:

- Ideals that guide or qualify personal conduct and interaction with others

- Help to distinguish what is right from what is wrong

- Determine conduct or _____

- Linked to and formative to your _____

- Linked to and formative to your _____

PERSONAL CORE VALUES

An Overview on Values

A well accepted definition of values is that they are ideals that guide or qualify personal conduct, interaction with others, and vocational involvement. Like morals, they help to distinguish what is right from what is wrong and provide information on how one can conduct their life in a meaningful way.

Values can be classified into four categories:

- Personal Values
- Cultural Values
- Social Values
- Work Values

Each person has built in "core" values that are predetermined valuations of God, self, others, things, tasks, concepts, ideas / opinions, concepts about your future and your role in the universe. Includes beliefs and internal positive and negative _____.

To discover your core values, you can take an online assessment called the Hartman Value Profile, which will measure your inner values landscape. The test reveals a report which provides an inventory that measures a person's capacity to make value judgments concerning the world (extrinsic) and one's self (intrinsic). You can learn more at **http://www.transcende.net** profile.

VALUES SCIENCE

Inner values are the foundation and boundaries for our Emotions and Thinking skills. These two then are acted out in our Behaviors.

Trust comes from behaving trustworthily, which ultimately comes from core values.

Values Science asserts that all behaviors come from how you THINK blended with your EMOTIONS. Thinking and emotions flow from your preset, core values. (For research and more information, see www.hartmaninstitute.org).

"As a man thinks in his heart, so is he." **Proverbs 23:7 (NKJV)**

VALUES SCIENCE

- **B = Behavior (Buoy):** above the surface (what we and others see) "the canvas upon which we paint our outward lives" - CAN BE MODIFIED!

- **Attitudes and Thinking**: Flex / stretch with rise and fall of circumstance - CAN CHANGE

- **V = Values**: Character, Spirit/Soul = Willpower, Choice Power - CAN BE CHANGED with:
  - Focus on one thing
  - Perseverance
  - Accountability
  - Word of God
  - . . . and time!

PRINCIPLE-BASED LEADERSHIP VALUES

B=Behavior; V=Values. They both can change over time and are both connected by your thinking and attitudes to your values. Values change very slowly and are the root of all human behavior.

- A posture – how you _____ yourself

- A mindset – fixed on Jesus and others

- A perspective (God, time, history, others)

- A discipline 24X7…with no off season

- An intentional Self- _____

VALUES SCIENCE

- Each person has built in "core" values that are predetermined valuations of God, self, others, things, tasks, concepts, ideas/opinions, concepts about your future and your role in the universe and beliefs.

- Hartman's Value theory proposes that "Good" is the degree in which your comparative valuation occurs in this hierarchy; People and self are always more valuable than things and tasks and these are always more valuable that ideas and concepts and dogma.

NOTES:

TABLE TALK

1. What kind of Core Values were you brought up with? Discuss.

2. How do these align with God's Values?

3. Is it better to ask "what would Jesus do?" or "Who would Jesus *be* (in this situation)?" Why?

CORE CONDITIONING

1. Meet together as a Squad offsite this week and finalize your deployment plan for the time between classes:

    a. Develop a service mission together that *"binds up the bruised or broken hearted," ..."sets the captive prisoners free" ...* or *"gives sight to the blind."*

    b. Do the service mission together as a team in the **next 3 weeks** and report to the class your experience.

2. Finish reading Called to War, Chapter 7

3. Read and then read Acts 1-4 and underline every occasion where you see the word "filled" and "power."

4. Read Ephesians 5:18-20

END OF SESSION

SESSION 6 — PART II: BLOWING YOUR OWN HORN

In the second part of Session 6 we will discuss attitudes and character, and how these traits relate to leadership.

ATTITUDES AND POWER

Judges 6:33 – 35

Now all the Midianites, Amalekites and other eastern peoples joined forces and crossed over the Jordan and camped in the Valley of Jezreel. Then the Spirit of the LORD came upon Gideon, and he blew a trumpet, summoning the Abiezrites to follow him. He sent messengers throughout Manasseh, calling them to arms, and also into Asher, Zebulun and Naphtali, so that they too went up to meet them.

> "Teachability and trust always leads to total obedience."
> - Ed Townsend

ATTITUDE ADJUSTMENTS OF GREAT LEADERS

- A leader must have an attitude of _____.

- _____ is made up of personal _____

   and accountability for others.

Personal accountability is an internal attitude that takes responsibility for their actions and not shift blame on others or circumstances. Personal time and resources are well managed.

Accountability for others is responsibility for the actions taken by those under their watch. It includes monitoring what they are doing and how they are doing it.

"He that would be the chief leader amongst you shall be the greatest servant for the first shall be last"

- Jesus Christ

"Let each of you look out not only for his own interests, but also for the interests of others. Let this mind be in you which was also in Christ Jesus, who, being in the form of God, did not consider it robbery to be equal with God, but made Himself of no reputation (kenosis-gk), taking the form of a bondservant, and coming in the likeness of men. And being found in appearance as a man, He humbled Himself and became obedient to the point of death, even the death of the cross. Therefore God also has highly exalted Him…"

- Philippians 2:4-9 (NKJV)

"Humility is closest to the heart of a leader who has the most accurate view of reality. Seeing things as they really are will create clear perspectives on the relative importance of the assets and resources at hand and the relative importance of the leader and each team member"

-- Art Hobba

- **"What did these leaders have in common?"**

TABLE TALK

1. Who is a Bible leader you admire most and why?

2. What kind of leader do you desire to be?

   What is the one thing you have to work on the most?

3. Pray for one another now as well as during the week, and expect to grow in that area so you can share next time at your table.

Principle-Based Leadership — "Power"

Gideon went from stranger to friend with God and enjoyed a personal relationship

- o He gave against the grain
- o He personally destroyed his idols
- o He consistently worshipped
- o He was given a new (True) name

God's Word was the basis of his power and anointing

1. *Then* the <u>Spirit of the LORD came upon Gideon (Your Name here)</u>

"Then"...followed after several faithful steps of

- o Obedience and Sacrificial worship
- o Overcoming fear

- o AND . . . 32,000 chose to follow him!

2. *He blew* a trumpet

- o Blew out his old air...Breathed in the Holy Spirit...blew out a note that carried many miles

- o *"The definitive measure of a leader's success is if they moved their people from where they were to where God wanted them to be."* - Henry Blackaby

3. Summoning the Abiezrites to *follow him*.

- o The definitive measure of a leader's success is if they moved their people from where they were to where God wanted them to be."

I am going to send you what my Father has promised; but stay in the city until you have been clothed with *power* from on high."   - Luke 24:49

But you will receive *power* when the Holy Spirit comes on you; and you will be my witnesses in Jerusalem, and in all Judea and Samaria, and to the ends of the earth." After he said this, he was taken up before their very eyes, and a cloud hid him from their sight.   - Acts 1:8

LEADERSHIP POWER

One Man's Story
As he found some success as an evangelist, he continually sought a greater connection and empowerment. During one of his earlier missions to the British Isles, he met a young Welsh Evangelist, Stephen Olford who had spiritual qualities he had longed for. "He had a dynamic...and exhilaration about him that I wanted to capture," said Billy.

After hearing Olford preach on being filled with the Holy Spirit, Billy approached him and said, "You've spoken of something that I don't have. I want the fullness of the Holy Spirit in my life too." Olford agreed to set aside two days . . . the two would talk and pray during the day, pausing long enough for Billy to preach at night.

Quite frankly, Olford said later, "His preaching was very ordinary". The crowd was small, passive and to Billy's invitation, and unresponsive. The next day, Olford continued the instruction, telling Billy he "must be broken", like the apostle Paul, letting God turn him inside out. "I gave him my testimony of how God completely turned my life inside out— and of experience of the Holy Spirit in his fullness and anointing," said Olford. "As I talked, those marvelous eyes glistened with tears, and he said, Stephen, I see it. That's what I want . . . ", and both men knelt and prayed on the floor. "I can still hear Billy pouring out his heart in a prayer of total dedication to the Lord," said Olford. "Finally, he (Billy) said,' My heart is so flooded with the Holy Spirit!' and we went from praying to praising...laughing and praising God, and Billy was walking back and forth in the room saying, 'I have it! I'm filled. This is a turning point in my life.'

That night, said Olford, "as Billy rose to speak, he was a man absolutely anointed." Members of the audience came forward to pray even before Billy gave an invitation. At the end of the sermon, practically the entire crowd rushed forward."

o Dr. Billy Graham called Stephen Olford *"the man who most influenced my ministry."* Billy Graham yearned for all of what God had for him and God met him right where he was as he sought him with all of his heart. He will do the same for you.

TABLE TALK

1. Are you filled with the Spirit today? If the Bible exhorts all believers to "**be** filled with the Spirit," how can we make this condition our *daily* experience?

   Brainstorm together.

2. Why do you think it is dangerous to step out into leadership alone?

   Prayer

   Lord Jesus. You told your followers to wait in Jerusalem to receive the powerful baptism of the Holy Spirit. I ask you now to give me all of what you have for me. Fill me to overflowing with the Holy Spirit. Hold nothing back. I surrender, yet again, to you."

   Thank you for the promise of the filling of the Spirit. I receive it now, by faith.

WRAP

- Decide now to take full responsibility for your success.

- Find a Mentor or a Coach…meet with them _____.

- Choose to continuously become more _____ - _____.

- Read the Bible through a "leadership lens."

- Study great _____.

- Read good leadership books.

- Purposefully lead, mentor and coach _____.

STEPPING INTO LEADERSHIP

DO NOT VENTURE ALONE!

Are you hearing the distant wind of the horn? Is the Spirit of God calling you to step out . . . to lead into a new realm of freedom for yourself and those who you care for?

The wisdom of Solomon teaches, *"Plans fail for lack of counsel, but with many advisers they succeed."* In Proverbs 15:22.

Share your thoughts and yearnings with Brothers at the table and then pray for God to confirm to you his next steps for you.

Share these confirmations with one another over the next few weeks and also with your wife (if married) and two or three close Brothers who know you.

CORE CONDITIONING

1. When you go to your rock every day this week, begin by thanking God for developing the leader in you and then ask Him to show you a leadership trait (one only) He wishes to grow or strengthen in you during this season.

   Pray about how Jesus would lead your:
   - Wife
   - Family
   - Ministry
   - Work

2. Read through chapter 9 of textbook.

END OF SESSION

SESSION 7:
TWELVE STRATEGIES FOR
DEFENSIVE WARFARE

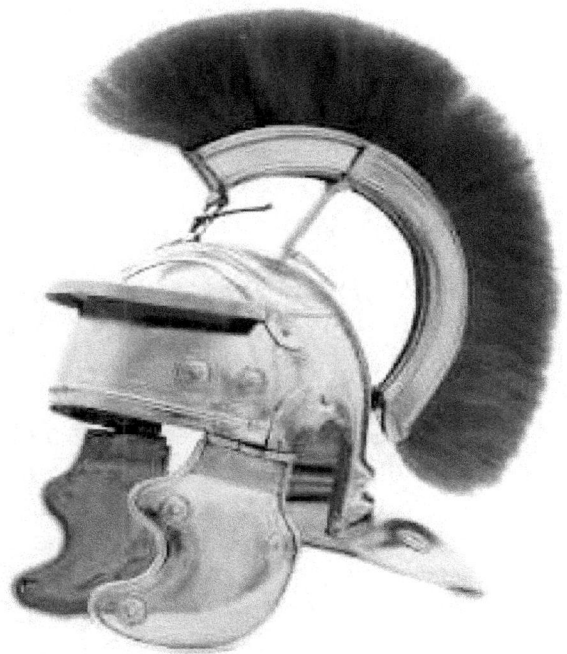

SESSION 7: PART 1 — TWELVE STRATEGIES FOR DEFENSIVE WARFARE

> ***Objective***
>
> The objective of this session is to understand the 12 strategies for defensive warfare. *"The best deterrent to warfare is a strong defense."*

GIDEON'S JOURNEY

The Battle Begins

> *"When I blow the trumpet, I and all who are with me, then you also blow the trumpets on every side of the whole camp, and say, **'The sword of the LORD and of Gideon!'"***

> *"So Gideon and the hundred men who were with him came to the outpost of the camp at the beginning of the middle watch, just as they had posted the watch; and they blew the trumpets and broke the pitchers that were in their hands. Then the three companies blew the trumpets and broke the pitchers—they held the torches in their left hands and the trumpets in their right hands for blowing—and they cried, "The sword of the LORD and of Gideon!" And every man stood in his place all around the camp; and the whole army ran and cried out and fled. When the three hundred blew the trumpets, **the LORD set every man's sword against his companion throughout the whole (enemy) camp**; and the army fled to Beth Acacia toward Zererah, as far as the border of Abel Meholah, by Tabbath."* (bold is mine)

Gideon had changed in a way that marked him for life. Many of you have read of men who have gone through this process in fiction and in real life. Frail, but ultimately faithful Men like Abraham, Joseph, Moses, and Daniel. Gideon's fire, however, was condensed and brilliant:

12 STRATEGIES FOR DEFENSIVE WARFARE

1. **The _____ of the Lord.**
   Combined with sincere love for God is oftentimes the core mental and emotional "fear of the Lord," or some form of that phrase, is used over 90 times in scripture. The unique thing about it, however, it is almost always presented as either a warning, exhortation, or a promise of God's protection and favor.

2. **Watchfulness – Judges 7:5-6**

   "Separate those who lap the water with their tongues like a dog from those who kneel down to drink." 6 Three hundred men lapped with their hands to their mouths. All the rest got down on their knees to drink.

   We are instructed in scripture to be wary of certain kinds of people, evil spirit beings, and the carnal and philosophical mindsets of the world system. Watchfulness can prevent untold evil attacks in our lives.

   "Watch and pray so that you will not fall into temptation. The spirit is willing, but the body is weak."
                                             --Jesus, to the disciples, in Matthew 26:41

3. **Trusting God**

   a. Not manipulation or testing God but

   b. Placing the full _____ of your faith in our Father creates:

         -release of His power
         -protection.

   We must placing the full weight of your faith in our Father will create a compelling release of God's heavenly power and protection. It is Daniel in the lions' den...David sprinting in descent into the arena of the valley to engage Goliath. And today, He still seeks for His children to step out of the boat, and to cast their cares upon Him in trusting abandon.

---

4. Confession

"Many Christians are unthinkably horrified when a real sinner is suddenly discovered among the righteous. So we remain alone with our sin, living alone in our lies and hypocrisy...he who is alone with his sins is utterly alone."

- Dietrich Bonhoeffer

"Therefore confess your sins to each other and pray for each other so that you may be healed."

- Apostle James, the Brother of Jesus

Epicenter of the Core 300 movement is the fearless commitment to _____ "what is said at the table, stays at the table."

The secret will get out- Jesus taught that it will be shouted "from the rooftops" of that which was done in secret.

5. Godly counsel

a. Relying upon the Word of Truth (Hebrews 4:12)

b. Hiding the Word in the "sheath of your heart" and meditating on scripture (Psalm 119:11, Proverbs 4:5-12).

c. The "threefold cord" that is not easily broken (Ecclesiastes 4:12)

d. The principle of safety in the midst of seeking plurality of wise input from wise believers for key decisions in our life (Proverbs 11:14)

6. Submission to _____ – READ these verses aloud

a. Government and Overseers	- Romans 13:1-3
b. Family and Marriage: Submission and Respect	- Ephesians 5
c. Government and Law	- Hebrews 13:17
d. Bosses and Employers	- I Peter 2:18-20
e. Church Leadership	- Hebrews 13:17
f. God (as our disciplining Father)	- James 4:7

Submit yourselves, then, to God. Resist the devil, and he will flee from you.

NOTE on Defensive Warfare: It is no accident that these two phrases are linked together! Submission sets the enemy to flight!

TABLE TALK

1. Everyone has some issues with authority. What are yours? Why do you think you have this kind of response? Does this affect your use of authority?

2. Has the women's movement affected your relationship with your wife? Do you ever find yourself compromising to please her or just keep the peace?

CORE CONDITIONING

1. Do a Scripture study in www.biblepathway.com by typing in "fear of the Lord" (exact phrase) and then read the verses. If they don't make sense expand the verse to take in the context. After this exercise, what does the "fear of the Lord" mean to you? Share your thoughts in your journal, this workbook.

2. It is a healthy thing to think about the limitations of submission in the church. How far does a Believer go in submission to biblical authority? How did the early church handle their interaction with government? Read the account of Ananias and Sapphira in Acts 5:1-10. If she submitted to her husband in the lie, why was she struck dead as well? Have a discussion about this with your wife, if married, tablemate, or with an elder/mentor/pastor in your life.

3. Read through chapter 10 of textbook

"He will be the sure foundation for your times, a rich store of salvation and wisdom and knowledge; the fear of the **LORD** is the key to this treasure." - Isaiah 33:6

END OF SESSION

SESSION 7 – PART 2: TWELVE STRATEGIES FOR DEFENSIVE WARFARE

In part two of this session, we will continue with learning the twelve strategies for defensive warfare.

*"When I blow the trumpet, I and all who are with me, then you also blow the trumpets on every side of the whole camp, and say, '**The sword of the LORD and of Gideon!**'"*

*"So Gideon and the hundred men who were with him came to the outpost of the camp at the beginning of the middle watch, just as they had posted the watch; and they blew the trumpets and broke the pitchers that were in their hands. Then the three companies blew the trumpets and broke the pitchers—they held the torches in their left hands and the trumpets in their right hands for blowing—and they cried, "The sword of the LORD and of Gideon!" And every man stood in his place all around the camp; and the whole army ran and cried out and fled. When the three hundred blew the trumpets, **the LORD set every man's sword against his companion throughout the whole (enemy) camp**; and the army fled to Beth Acacia toward Zererah, as far as the border of Abel Meholah, by Tabbath."* (bold is mine)

"The best deterrent to warfare is a strong defense"
                                                                              --Ronald Reagan

7. Cultivate a Praise and _____ Lifestyle

a. Gideon's example

b. Verbally singing and/or glorifying God causes two things to occur:

1) God's habitation . . . his very presence, enters the place where you worship Him.

2) God will release confusion and destruction upon enemy forces around us as we exalt His name out loud.

3) Has the healthy effect of "blowing out the pipes" of your soul as worship flows from your heart into the heavens towards "Him who sits on the Throne!"

WORSHIP LAB

Most men do not know how to praise God out loud without reading from Psalms or singing (if at all) from a hymnal or video screen.

Yet it is **commanded** by scripture because a powerful freedom is released in a man's life when he opens his mouth in praise.

RIGHT NOW, Practice together, in unison speaking out these words boldly together in your class. Do it 3-4 times in the atmosphere of worship…no music needed!

8. Honoring your parents

This is the first commandment with an attached blessing. It releases God's blessing on you for both an extended life and personal wellness (Deuteronomy 5:16).

NOTE: How you treat your folks will have an impact on how your children treat you in your later years.

9. Never _____ your enemy

"There is no greater disaster than underestimating your enemy"
-- **Tao Te Ching**, Lao Tzu

Foreknowledge cannot be inferred from comparison of previous events, or from the calculations of the heavens, but must be obtained from people who have knowledge of the enemy's situation.

--Sun-Tzu, The Art of War

a. Jesus knew His enemy well and so should we.

b. The enemy is you; a system; and a *person*.

c. The devil is _____. He orchestrates of the three dimensions of evil

d. Source of Philosophies within and outside the church

e. He is a counterfeiter with no original powers other than feint, fear and

_____

REAL VS. COUNTERFEIT

REAL VS. COUNTERFEIT

God	Satan
Truth	Half Truths
Motivate	Manipulate
Love	Lust
Passion	Drivenness
Anger	Rage
Rest	Escape
Celebrate	Party Spirit
Distrust	Bitterness
Courage	Bravado
Beautiful	Brazen
Wisdom	Craftiness
Inspire	Intimidate
Release	Control

Copyright © 2009 Art Hobba

Interactive group question: Can anyone name some other God vs. Satan opposites?

Some of the names used in scripture for Satan are:

Adversary (1 Peter 5:8); The Devil (Ephesians 6:11) The Deceiver; The Wicked One (Matthew 13:19, 38); Baalzebub (Matt 10:25; 12:24); Liar, Father of lies (John 8:44); Murderer from the beginning (John 8:44); The Dragon (Isaiah 51:9); The Lion-Devourer (Malachi 3:11; I Peter 5:8); The Prince of this World (John 12:31); the Prince of the Power of the Air (Ephesians 2:2; 6:12); Lucifer (Isaiah 14:12); Angel of Light (2 Corinthians 11:14); The god of this World (2 Corinthians 4:4); The Accuser of the Brethren (Revelations 12:10); The Enemy (Matthew 13:39); The Serpent (Genesis 3:1); The Tempter (Matt 4:3).

10. Remembering our mission – To become _____ Jesus Christ
Let us fix our eyes on Jesus, the author and perfector of our faith, who for the joy set before him endured the cross, scorning its shame, and sat down at the right hand of the throne of God…In your struggle against sin, you have not yet resisted to the point of shedding your blood…Endure hardship as discipline; God is treating you as sons. For what son is not disciplined by his father?...God disciplines us for our good, that we may share in his holiness. ¹¹No discipline seems pleasant at the time, but painful. Later on, however, it produces a harvest of righteousness and peace for those who have been trained by it."

Hebrews 12:2-13 (partial)

11. Man can often be the _____ of the enemy

a. Yourself – Self-awareness mandates that you do not blindly follow your heart
    NOTE: Tell a personal story here where you became a threat to God's peace, harmony, safety or love in *your* family

b. Others

"But Jesus did not commit Himself to them, because He knew all men, ²⁵ and had no need that anyone should testify of man, for He knew what was in man."
-- *John 2:24-25*

"These six things the LORD hates, Yes, seven are an abomination to Him: A false witness who speaks lies, And one who sows discord among brethren."

NOTES:

12. Keep the Divine _____.

> The
> *mountaintop.*
> Down on the battle
> field, everything is
> smoke and confusion. It is
> hard to tell friend from foe,
> to see who is winning, to foresee
> the enemy's next move. The general
> must climb high above the fray, to the
> mountaintop, where everything becomes
> clearer and more in focus. There he can see
> beyond the battlefield --- to the movements of
> reserves; to the enemy camp, to the battles future shape.
> Only from the mountaintop can the general direct the war.
> **--Robert Greene**

TABLE TALK

1. Think about a recent event in your life where things "hit the fan," or you or family member were seriously hurt by others or adverse circumstances. Share the story briefly with your Squad. Discuss whether that event may have been an orchestrated attack of the enemy.

2. What new steps can you take going forward to provide for a better hedge of defensive protection for you? How can you use of your 911 to reduce your risk of attack?

CORE CONDITIONING

Reading:

- Read Ephesians 6:10-18, Isaiah 59:16-18, Revelation 19:11-19.

- Call your 911 and discuss:

    - Why do you think Gideon totally annihilated every Midianite on earth?

    - How does this apply to your adversary and your *"Game Face?"*

- Read Chapters 1 of "Called to War."

END OF SESSION

SESSION 8:
PUTTING ON THE BODY ARMOR

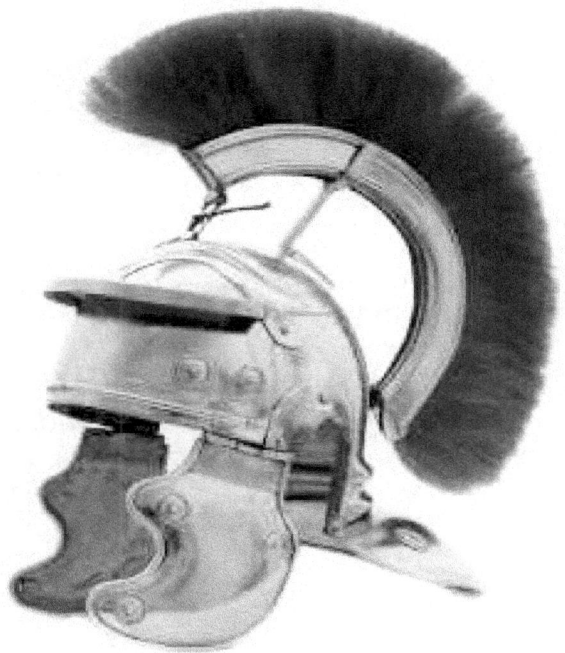

SESSION 8: PART 1 — PUTTING ON THE BODY ARMOR

Objective

The objective of this session is to the various elements of the Body Armor and how we effectively use them.

"Integrity is who you are when no one is looking."

- Anonymous

Warriors in training

"Therefore put on the full armor of God, so that when the day of evil comes, you may be able to stand your ground, and after you have done everything, to stand. Stand firm then, with the belt of truth buckled around your waist, with the breastplate of righteousness in place, and with your feet fitted with the readiness that comes from the gospel of peace."

- Ephesians 6:13-15

Who is this King of glory?
The LORD strong and mighty,
The LORD mighty in battle.

- Psalm 24:8

ROMAN ARMY CIRCA 64 A.D.

Overview

Gaius Marius - proconsul in Rome in 107 B.C. is credited with transforming the Roman

Army into a _____ __ _____.

- Paved the way for the expansion of the Roman Empire

- Standardized training

- Year round drilling and skills development

- Developed common uniforms and weaponry

WHO ARE YOU?

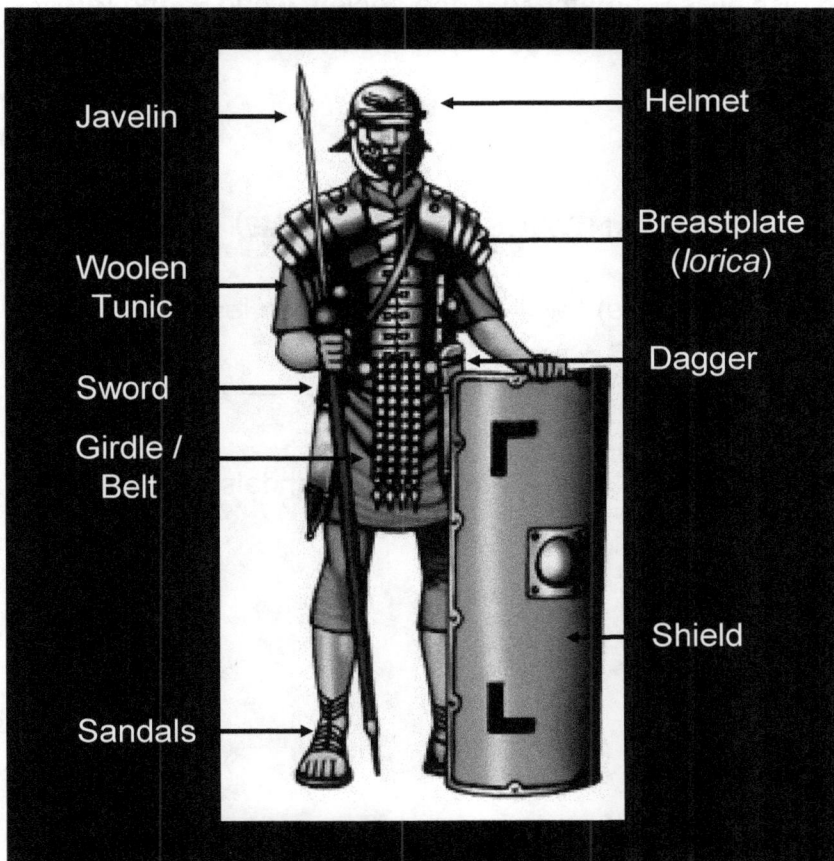

Javelin — Helmet

Woolen Tunic — Breastplate (*lorica*)

Sword — Dagger

Girdle / Belt

Sandals — Shield

The body armor of the Roman foot soldier was designed for:

- Mobility and Protection.

- Comfort for long marches

The Legion was organized as follows:

- 6,000 men of whom 5,200 were actual soldiers

- 10 cohorts of 6 "Centuries" each

- 1 Century contained 80 men.

- Divided into 8 man units, or squads, called a *contubernia*.

The **Century** led by a Centurion officer, fought as a _____, marched as a unit, and camped as a unit. The soldiers and officers, who are frequently mentioned in the pages of the Gospels and other New Testament writings, were trained rigorously to peak physical condition and discipline, unmatched in the ancient world....and rarely seen today.

ROMAN ARMOR (SANDALS – CALIGAE)

- **The sandals** (*caligae*) - well-ventilated, strong leather sandals with leather straps

- Iron Hob nails in the soles for _____ and to be more hard-wearing.

- They were well-ventilated, strong leather sandals with leather straps.

GOSPEL OF PEACE

Dem Gospel Shoes

John Wooden took the first part of the first day of practice to train his basketball players how to care for and put on their shoes

- Gospel Shoes are a metaphor for our stance, our foundation and our role of Kingdom

    _____.

- Jesus came preaching the "gospel of the Kingdom" and Paul thinks of these military shoes as the foundation of what is needed to **take redemptive ground for the King.**

- Adam's rulership of the earth

    *Then God said, "Let us make man in our image, in our likeness, and let them **rule** over the fish of the sea and the birds of the air, over the livestock, **over all the earth,** and over all the creatures that move along the ground." So God created man in his own image, in the image of God he created him; male and female he created them. God blessed them and said to them, "Be fruitful and increase in number; fill the earth and **subdue it. Rule over** the fish of the sea and the birds of the air and over every living creature that moves on the ground." Genesis 1:26-28*

- Abraham's inheritance: Abraham, similarly, was given a land of promise to him and his descendants.

    "The LORD said to Abram, "Lift up your eyes from where you are and look north and south, east and west. All the land that you see I will give to you and your offspring [a] forever. [16] I will make your offspring like the dust of the earth, so that if anyone could count the dust, then your offspring could be counted. Go, walk through the length and breadth of the land, for I am giving it to you."

    Genesis 13:14-17

Roman soldiers had a "_____" attitude. Their foot declared the presence of the order of the Pax Romana and power of Caesar's government

ROMAN ARMOR (THE LEATHER GIRDLE-BELT)

The leather girdle-skirt (*Pterugres*) was the _____ of physical fitness and battle balance. Also is symbolic of our place of greatest vulnerability as a man

    a. The loincloth- to put on _____ "gird up the loins of your mind"

    Therefore gird up the loins of your mind, be sober, and rest your hope fully upon the grace that is to be brought to you at the revelation of Jesus Christ; as obedient children, not conforming yourselves to the former lusts, as in your ignorance;
                                       -- I Peter 1:13-14, NKJV

    It defines the "loins" as: the place where the Hebrews thought the generative power (semen) resided

    b. The heavy leather skirt that was cut into strips and studded with iron for protection of the lower belly and upper legs.

    c. **The sheaths** for the dagger and _____

"**Gird up**" represents:

- Action of a warrior preparing for a battle. In the Old Testament (I Samuel 25:13; Psalm 45:3)

- A sense of hurriedness and fear

- The need for vigilant *readiness* and *action*.

- Source of the "_____ _____" and guts

ROMAN ARMOR (THE HELMET — GALEA)

- Made of Iron
- Simple upside down bowl-like design
- Flexible leather cheek and ear coverings
- Weighed 11-13 pounds
- Serious training issues due to weight and mobility
- Wool or quilted inside structure

THE HELMET OF SALVATION

- Under the Helmet is the mind of _____ A "Christian world view" = Christ's worldview Meditating on His word (so I might not sin against thee)

- Under the Helmet is Holy Spirit's _____ of the ways of Satan

  What enables the enlightened rulers and good generals to conquer the enemy at every move and achieve extraordinary success is foreknowledge."   -- Sun Tzu, The Art of War

- Under the Helmet is _____, clarity and Kingdom peace

  "And the peace of God, which transcends all understanding, will guard your hearts and your minds in Christ Jesus. Finally, brothers, whatever is true, whatever is noble, whatever is right, whatever is pure, whatever is lovely, whatever is admirable—if anything is excellent or praiseworthy—think about such things. Whatever you have learned or received or heard from me, or seen in me—put it into practice. And the God of peace will be with you."

- Under the Helmet is Mental _____

  "And the things that you have heard from me among many witnesses, commit these to faithful men who will be able to teach others also. You therefore must endure hardship as a good soldier of Jesus Christ. "   2 Timothy 2:3

- Under the Helmet is _____ - _____

  No one engaged in warfare entangles himself with the affairs of this life, that he may please him who enlisted him as a soldier."   2 Timothy 2:4

"He who doubts is like a wave of the sea, blown and tossed by the wind. That man should not think he will receive anything from the Lord; he is a double-minded man, unstable in all he does."   James 1:6b-8

THE HELMET OF SALVATION

- Under the Helmet is _____ to your Commanding Officer

    The temptation to be armored up, dangerous and then take off on your own adventur is very real for men. We must realize the strength of an army is in its unified coordination under the command, not I any individual's ability to fight.

    Jesus is our example here when, under profound temptation to bail on His mission, H told the Father, "Not My will, but Your will be done."

- Putting on the helmet is a _____ to submit to God and His authorities in your life.

After the English had captured the leader of the Scottish army, William Wallace, we see him stretched out on a rack in a public square. His love (Isabella) runs to his side pleading for hi to swear his allegiance to the evil King Edward I (Longshanks) in order to avoid the pending torturous dismemberment of his bowels:

Reading from the end of **Braveheart**:

> *Isabella: Sir, I've come to beg you to confess all and swear allegiance to the king, tha he might show you mercy.*
> *William: Will he show mercy to my country?*
> *Isabella: Mercy is to die quickly, perhaps even live in a tower. In time, who knows wh could happen.*
> *William: If I swear to him, then all that I am is dead already.*
> *Isabella: You will die. It will be awful.*
> *William: Every man dies, not every man really lives.*
> *Isabella: Drink this. It will dull your pain.*
> *William: No. It will numb my wits, and I must have them all. For if I'm senseless or if wail, then Longshanks will have broken me.*
> *(long pause)*
> *William: I am so afraid. Give me the strength to die well.*

TABLE TALK

1. How has "whacked" values or sick thinking caused pain to you and others? How does that reflect on your attitude towards the Helmet of Salvation?

2. Gideon's doubts about God's Word to him caused him to test God twice (fleeces). How is this related to putting on the Helmet of Salvation as a leader?

One of the warriors of old made this statement: "The purpose of war is victory, and the purpose of victory is occupation." In the Kingdom, we add one more step to the process: The purpose of occupation is expansion.

It's important that we view life with the perspective of expansion and forward motion. It's not healthy to simply find a place you want to stay in and occupy. The moment you have found a leveling-off place is the moment you begin backsliding.

When your passion begins to decline, you already start to die. You were born to burn. When leaders don't have passion, it costs everyone who follows.

Passion and the anointing run in parallel courses. A person with passion will take risks. Everything you want in the realm of the Kingdom is found through this veil of difficulty by stepping into the realm of inconvenience. You don't get it by coasting on yesterday's breakthrough. You were born for expansion.

From Occupation to Expansion, by Bill Johnson

NOTES:

CORE CONDITIONING — PREPARING FOR DEPLOYMENT

1. Begin to daily ask God where He wants your table to be deployed after bootcamp. If married or if you have kids, invite them into the prayer as well.

2. Meet with your mission director (can be delegated to 2 guys at your table) or Pastor and ask him/her about some of the heartfelt service opportunities there are in the church or the local community right now that are not being met (and don't shy away from men teaching Sunday School!).

3. Research online (can be delegated to 2-3 different guys in your table) and community several key pain points/needs where a few good men could make a difference.

4. Bring your ideas to your table next week and then calendar a time to meet offsite t seek God as to what your Squad is called to do as He deploys you after you get your coin.

SESSION 8 – PART 2: PUTTING ON THE BODY ARMOR

In part 2 of this session we will continue to discuss the various pieces of body armor.

ROMAN ARMOR (THE BREASTPLATE – LORICA)

The "*lorica laminate*" was the core protection of the common centurion-led, foot soldier shows how it was made of many horizontal metal (iron) plates layered over each other and tied together by internal straps made of animal skin. The armor itself consisted of broad ferrous iron strips ('girth hoops') fastened to the strips were arranged horizontally on the body and they surrounded the torso in two halves, being fastened at the sides to protect the front and back.

Paul n*ever saw* the Hollywood's popular "muscles" version

- Laminated with layers of horizontal iron plates

- Surrounded the entire torso…360 degrees

- Added trained body weight in the field

- Created a sense of freedom, fearlessness and _____ in battle

- Center of Integrity of the soldiers complete readiness

THE BREASTPLATE OF RIGHTEOUSNESS

Overlapping _____ of righteousness men need to wear every day

- Washed before the throne of God

- Openness before God and men

- Humility that without the breastplate we are toast

- Forgiving heart towards self and others

- Integrity upholds us and gives confidence

"The integrity of the upright guides them, but the unfaithful are destroyed by their duplicity.
                              - Proverbs 11:3

The breastplate of righteousness *covers the heart* of the forgiven and forgiving man. To wa[l]k into battle without having forgiven all others who have harmed you is unwise. To engage th[e] adversary, not knowing the confident clarity, and the refreshment of soul, that comes with being personally cleansed with God's forgiveness, can disable the covering and protection [of] His righteousness as well.

Many of the battles we lose may have been waged in our hearts and souls for many years.

NOTES:

THE BREASTPLATE OF RIGHTEOUSNESS

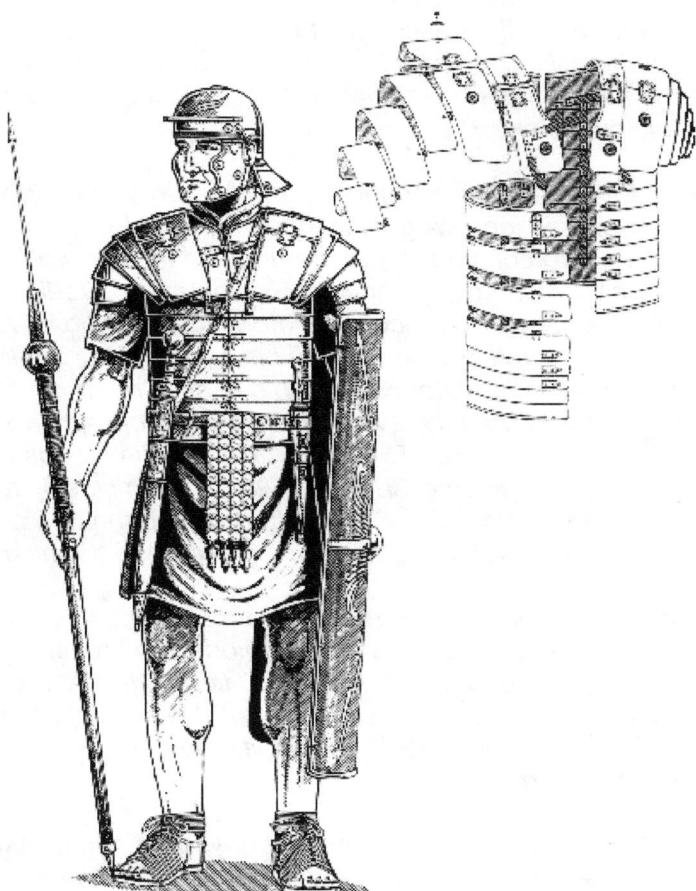

The _____ of bitterness or unforgiveness will weaken your breastplate and open up your vital pars to destruction

The condition of an unforgiving heart is a very common condition of Hells strategies. We must therefore guard and test our hearts against men, and that inner condition of unforgiveness that can put you on the "injured reserved" list before the battle campaign ever begins.

NOTES:

REMARKS AT JSCOPE 2000, JANUARY 27, 2000
By General Charles C. Krulak, USMC (Retired)

Sound morals cut to the heart and soul of who we are and what we are and what we must be. men and women of character. They arm us for the challenges to come and impart to us a sense of wholeness. They unite us in the calling we now know as the profession of arms. Of all the moral and ethical guideposts, the one that I have kept in the forefront of my mind . . . is integrity. It is my ethical and personal touchstone.

Integrity, as we know it today, stands for soundness of principle and character – uprightness-honesty. Yet there is more. Integrity is also an ideal. A goal to strive for. And for a man or woman to "walk in their integrity" is to require constant discipline and usage. The word integrity itself is a martial word that comes to us from an ancient Roman army. Tradition durin the time of the twelve Caesars, the Roman army would conduct morning inspections. As the inspecting Centurion would come in front of each Legionnaire (in his century), the soldier would strike with his right fist the armor breastplate that covered his heart. The armor had to be strongest there in order to protect the heart from the sword thrusts and from arrow strikes. As the soldier struck his armor, he would shout "INTEGRITAS," which in Latin means materia wholeness, completeness and entirety. The inspecting Centurion would listen closely for this affirmation and also for the ring that well kept armor would give off. Satisfied that the armor was sound and that the soldier beneath it was protected, he would move on to the next man.

At about the same time, the Praetorians or imperial bodyguard were ascending into power an influence. Drawn from the best "politically correct" soldiers of the legions, they received the finest equipment and armor. They no longer had to shout "integritas" to signify that their armo was sound. Instead, as they struck their breastplate, they would shout "Hail Caesar," to signif that their heart belonged to the imperial personage – not to their unit –they armored themselves to serve the cause of a single man.

A century passed and the rift between the legion and the imperial bodyguard and its excesse grew larger. His standards and morals were high. He was not associated with the immoral conduct that was rapidly becoming the signature of the Praetorian Guards.

The armor of integrity continued to serve the Legion well for over four centuries. But by 383 AD, the social decline that infected the Republic and the Praetorian Guard had its effects upo the Legion. As a 4th Century Roman general wrote,

"When, because of negligence and laziness, parade ground drills were abandoned, the customary armor began to feel heavy since the soldiers rarely, if ever, wore it. Therefore, the first asked the Emperor to set aside the breastplates and mail. Then the helmets. So our soldiers fought the Goths without any protection for the heart and head and were often beate by archers. They took their armor off, and when the armor came off, so too came their integrity." It was only a matter of a few years until the legion rotted from within and was unabl to hold the frontiers. The barbarians were at the gates.

TABLE TALK

1. What is your forgiveness process?

2. What is the condition of your integrity? How can mutual encouragement, fellowshipping with other warrior disciples and locking shields in prayer help you keep your "*integritas*?"

ROMAN ARMOR (FINAL THOUGHT)

The purpose and design of the armor was NOT for peacekeeping, but to equip men for conquest of new lands . . . to engage and fight; to win the day; and to seize new hostile territory for the Emperor's domain.

NOTES:

CORE CONDITIONING

Reading:

- Finish Judges 7 and 8

- Finish Text "Called to War"

- Contemplation:

- Why do you think Gideon totally annihilated every Midianite on earth?

- How does this apply to your adversary and your *"Game Face?"*

END OF SESSION

Session 9:
Total Annihilation

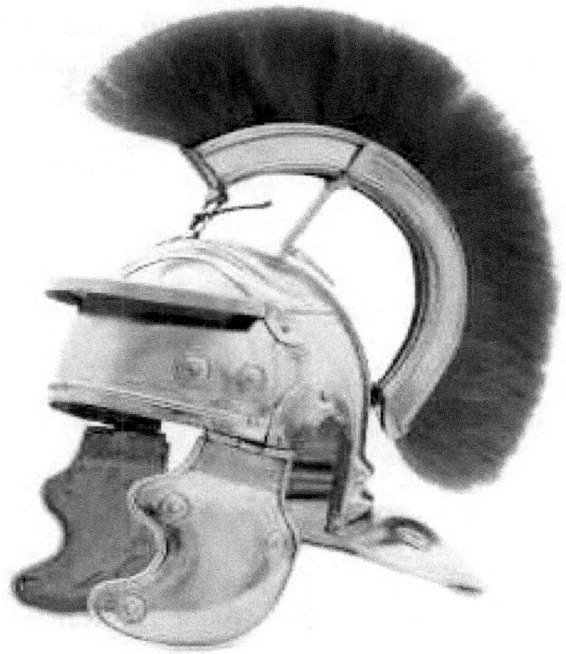

SESSION 9: TOTAL ANNIHILATION

Objective

The objective of this session is to continue to address the various elements of the Body Armor and how we effectively use them, specifically the Sword and Shield.

"But You say let it go, You say let it go,
You say life is waiting for the ones who lose control
You say you will be everything I need
You say if I lose my life it's then I find my soul"

-- Tenth Avenue North

EPHESIANS 6:16-18

Warriors in training

"In addition to all this, take up the shield of faith, with which you can extinguish _____ the flaming arrows of the evil one.

Take the helmet of salvation and the sword of the Spirit, which is the word of God. And **pray** in the Spirit on all occasions with all kinds of prayers and requests . . ."

Roman Armor (Care and Maintenance)

You have loved righteousness and hated wickedness; therefore God, your God, has set you above your companions by anointing you with the oil of joy."

-- Hebrews 1:9

ILLUSTRATION:

An auto in disrepair; I assume it is unreliable and judge the owner as one who either has no affection for he car nor a sense of stewardship for it. He is often judged as undisciplined in his life or poor. We all know how badly we can get in trouble when our car breaks down. How much worse the poorly trained, poorly nourished and poorly equipped soldier. No wonder we lose so many personal battles and do know how to stand together!

The simplest form of care for the armor was to **keep it dry**, in good repair, clean and keep the metal components **well oiled**. Appearance was secondary, but important in much the same way today that most guys I know will apologize if I have to get into their car and it is dirty or cluttered or runs poorly.

- **A chafing girdle** and helmet (leather liner) causes painful rashes or instable support

- **Rusty plates of the breast-armor** will limit movement or open them up to injury.

- **A dull sword**

- **A weakened shield** from continual use and not reinforced, it could give way in battle

ROMAN ARMOR (CARE AND MAINTENANCE)

Like a well maintained car, *the oiling* of all of the moving parts is critical.

We know that anointing with oil . . .

    = filling and overflowing of the Spirit

    = _____ medicine

    = God's presence

    = _____ and enabling of God

    = loving united fellowship

The leather girdle-skirt (Pterugres) was oiled to keep it soft and comfortable...and *flexible* for action.

The sandals (caligae) had hob nails embedded in the soles for traction and durability and need oiling for comfort and to prevent rust.

NOTES:

BATTLE READINESS

> *"How good and pleasant it is when brothers live together in unity! It is like precious oil poured on the head, running down on the beard, running down on Aaron's beard, down upon the collar of his robes."*
>
> *-- King David the Warrior, Psalm 133:1-2*

> *"They set the tables, they spread the rugs, they eat, (Be well fed with the Word of God to fight!) they drink (of Christ's essence of Living Water)! Get up, you officers, **oil the shields!"***
>
> *-- Isaiah 21:5*

All of these metaphors have application for the well armed man of God.

ROMAN ARMOR (THE SWORD - GLADIUS)

Carried at the waist with a support strap around the shoulder and girded to the loins in the scabbard.

- Typically a two-edged sword for cutting.

- The Gladiator (swordsmen) was named after this weapon.

- The owners name, especially if a high-ranking official, was usually engraved on the blade.

THE SWORD OF THE SPIRIT

Identified by Paul as the _____ of God.

- **A well oiled, _____ sword** was an effective instrument of both death and protection.

   "Are you Sharp in the Word?"

- Tempered (made strong) in _____ by the **Sword Smith**

Heb 4:12-13 *"For the word of God is living and powerful, and sharper than any two-edged sword, piercing even to the division of soul and spirit, and of joints and marrow, and is a discerner of the thoughts and intents of the heart. [13] And there is no creature hidden from His sight, but all things are **NAKED** and **OPEN** to the eyes of Him to whom we must give account." (NKJV)*

- Naked and Open = make vulnerable by pulling back the neck and exposing to the knife

NOTES:

TABLE TALK

1. How has God allowed *circumstances* to temper you "by fire?" How did you change in the process?

2. How has He used *people* to sharpen His Word's activity in your heart?

NOTE: The "Sword Smith" is Christ through the Holy Spirit. He uses imperfect people, trials, and the fellowship of His suffering to make us be strong, resilient, sharp and dangerous!

CORE CONDITIONING

1. Pray about what is next for you and your Squad.

2. Meet together as a Squad this week and begin planning for the weeks and months between classes:|

   a. How/where to continue to meet regularly as a small group...maybe even plan a family event?

   b. Develop a service project or mission together that "binds up he bruised or broken hearted," "sets the captive prisoners free" or "gives sight to the blind."

SESSION 9 – PART 2: TOTAL ANNIHILATION

In part 2 of this session we will continue to discuss the purposes of the sword.

THE SWORD OF THE SPIRIT (FIVE PURPOSES)

1. The _____ **of Truth – Hebrews 4:12-13**

> *"For the word of God is living and powerful, and sharper than any two-edged sword, piercing even to the division of soul and spirit, and of joints and marrow, and is a discerner of the thoughts and intents of the heart.* [13] *And there is no creature hidden from His sight, but all things are naked and open to the eyes of Him to whom we mus[t] give account."* (NKJV)

NOTE: First used on yourself…and then for the healing and deliverance others

2. Field Rations – the Word of God is the _____ of Life

You may have the heard the one about the old Alaskan tradesman in Anchorage in the late 1890's who had two massive work dogs. During the day they would haul loa[d] of wood around his shop and into town, pulling a flatbed wooden sled.

One of the dogs, a blend of husky and wolf was pure white with blue eyes. The other was a Mastiff mix and was mostly black. Most Saturday nights, he would go to town for the weekly dog fights and many times place a bet on both his white dog and his black dog. Sometimes it as for them to win…others it for them to lose, but the patter[n] was different for each time.

One Monday morning the charcoal man arrived to make his weekly delivery, but this time, instead of exchanging the coal for the tradesman's money and leaving, he had ask a question that had been bothering him for weeks. He has been to most of the d[og] fights and seen the old man's dogs win and lose, but it bugged him that the old man always seemed to win the bet…whether his dog won or lost the match.

"How do you always seem to know whether your dog is going to win or lose," he asked. Well I'll tell you if you swear to never tell another soul, said the old man. "Agreed, said the man, his curiosity rising, "and here's my hand on it." And they shoo[k]

The tradesman broke a thin smile and cocked his head to the left and said, "You see, they are both great fighters, but whichever one I feed that week, usually wins."

The story illustrates a powerful yet simple truth:

If you feed your spirit with *daily* portions of the Word of God and commune with Jesus Christ, the living Bread of Life, your soul, already called by God to be a Mighty Warrior, will win. Starve the Warrior of his Living Bread...lose the battle. Starve him long enough, and you'll lose the war.

3. As the instrument of health and healing

*From the fruit of his mouth a man's stomach is filled; with the harvest from his lips he is satisfied. The tongue has the **power of life and death**, and those who love it will eat its fruit. --Proverbs 18:20-22*

*He **sent** forth **his word** and **healed** them; he rescued them from the grave. --Psalms 107:20*

4. The bringer of _____ (deliverance)

Let the saints rejoice in this honor and sing for joy on their beds. May the praise of God be in their mouths and a double-edged sword in their hands, to inflict vengeance on the nations and punishment on the people?

-- Psalm 149:5-7

Gideon's men lifted their battle cry; "The sword of the Lord and the sword of Gideon!"

The most common kind of miracle performed by Jesus was delivering men, woman, and children from demons. Today, most churches have purposely avoided the subject of the demonization of human beings. Frankly, it scares most of us.

Therefore God exalted him to the highest place and gave him the name that is above every name, that at the name of Jesus every knee should bow, in heaven and on earth and under the earth, and every tongue confess that Jesus Christ is Lord, to the glory of God the Father
-Philippians 2:9-11

"You believe that there is one God. You do well. Even the demons believe —and tremble!"

--James 2:19 NKJV

God, who made an open display over all demonic powers when he raised Christ from the dead, "triumphing over them

- The word for **tremble** here is the Latin word _____, the root of horrified:

    = freezing in their steps,

    = unable to respond or

    = unable to breath due to paralyzing fear

- The demons _____ Jesus not to torment them (Matthew 8:29)

God, who made an open display over all demonic powers when he raised Christ from the dead, "triumphing over them" has the full expectation that we will not default on what He has placed in us when we received Christ and became triumphant sons and daughters of God.

"He called his twelve disciples to him and gave them authority to drive out evil spirits and to heal every disease and sickness

-- Matthew 10:1

5. Represents the return of the King (Revelation 19)

- Total Annihilation and no _____

"When the LORD your God brings you into the land you are entering to possess and drives out before you many nations—the Hittites, Girgashites, Amorites, Canaanites, Perizzites, Hivites and Jebusites, seven nations larger and stronger than you- [2] *and when the LORD your God has delivered them over to you and you have defeated them, then* **you must destroy them totally**. *Make no treaty with them, and* **show them no mercy**....*This is what you are to do to them: Break down* **their** *altars, smash their sacred stones, cut down their Asherah poles and burn their idols in the fire" Deut 7:1-7*

Excalibur, Sword of Aragon (Tolkien), Knighthood

"A sword for the LORD and for Gideon!" Judges 7:20

NOTES:

ROMAN ARMOR (THE SHIELD — SCUTUM)

The shield had layered, external leather covering which needed oiling to keep it from becoming hard or brittle and prevent cracking.

- The curved shape of the shield allowed it to absorb heavy blows.

- The shield was constructed of hardwood covered over with leather and was sometimes trimmed with metal edges. A weapon in itself, it could sometimes stun or kill an opponent.

- The shape of the shield (50" H x 25" W) allowed packed formations of legionaries to overlap their shields, protecting each other and forming a moving and sometimes unstoppable wall.

"They set the tables, they spread the rugs, they eat, they drink! Get up, you officers, oil the shields!"

--Isaiah 21:5

THE SHIELD OF FAITH

- Represents _____ in your stance.

- Quenches the fiery darts
  - Words planted in our mind
  - Ghosts of our past

- Fears of the present and future
  - Voices of accusers and gossips

- Deflects the blows of Hell

- Drives the sled into enemy territory

YOUR LEADERSHIP LEGACY

Judges 8:28

"Thus Midian was subdued before the Israelites and did not raise its head again.

During Gideon's lifetime, the land enjoyed peace forty years."

TABLE TALK

1. How many ways can you think of to protect your 911 with your shield?

2. Why do you think Gideon totally annihilated every Midianite on earth? How does this apply to your "Game Face regarding he Baal's and Asherah's in your life?"

CORE CONDITIONING / END OF SESSION

NOTE: This Warrior course was in part, brought to you by the foresight and generosity of other brothers in Christ.

If you and your men have been freed and empowered through his study, please consider asking the men to prepare to *bring an offering next week* for Core 300.

Revelation 1:17

"I saw heaven standing open and there before me was a white horse, whose rider is called Faithful and True. With justice he judges and makes war. His eyes are like blazing fire, and on his head are many crowns. He has a name written on him that no one knows but he himself. He is dressed in a robe dipped in blood, and his name is the Word of God. The armies of heaven were following him, riding on white horses and dressed in fine linen, white and clean. Out of his mouth comes a sharp sword with which to strike down the nations. "He will rule them with an iron scepter." He treads the winepress of the fury of the wrath of God Almighty. On his robe and on his thigh he has this name written:

KING OF KINGS AND LORD OF LORDS.

Putting on the Armor - Stand

"Lord, I need Your help and protection in the battles I face against the World, the devil and my own sinful nature. I need Your armor and Your Sword and Shield. I choose to be Your warrior and to follow you as my Captain-King. I will not go out alone but will join with others in my mission of advancing the Kingdom of God.

By faith, I gird my core up with Truth.

By faith, I put on the Shoes as an Ambassador of the good news of Your Kingdom

By faith, and because I am forgiven and holy before You, I put on the Breastplates of Righteousness

By faith, because I have been given Your spiritual mind, I put on the Helmet of Salvation Then Lord, I take up the shield of Your faithfulness and the Sword of Your living, powerful spirit. I am more than a Conqueror. Thank You for the Victory!

PLEASE NOTE:

1. Make sure any missed classes are watched and that you take notes while viewing videos available at www.core300.org/videos Go to and select the class you may have missed

2. Finish reading all of the textbook, **Called to War** if you have not done so by now.

3. **Integritas Moment** -Please let your Squad Leader know if you have completed #1 and #2 above. Until they are finished, you may go through the ceremony but should postpone the reception of your coin. Your Squad Leader will keep it for you and convey it at the appropriate time.

AMEN!

Session 10:
The Armor of God
Coin Conveyance
Ceremony and
Celebration

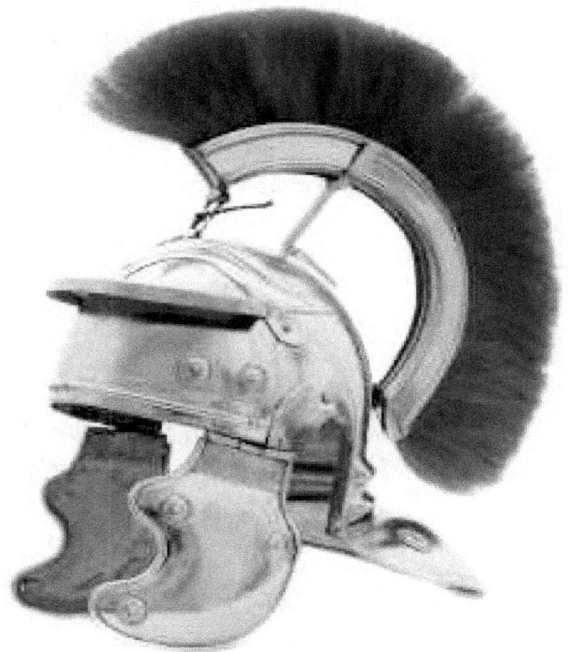

SESSION 10: ARMOR OF GOD CONVEYANCE CEREMONY

GIDEON'S LEGACY

- Alone, hiding and disqualified

- He gave sacrificially of his blood on the floor

- He worshipped God 4 times and built 3 altars

- He obeyed God in harms way by pulling down the stronghold of Baal and destroying the Asherah pole, restoring pure worship to his village and nation

- He faltered in his faith but then called the men to follow him into battle

- God has equipped us as mighty warriors with the Armor of God

- He totally annihilated 200,000 warriors with 300 mighty men

- He brought peace and prosperity to Israel for 40 years

"Thus Midian was subdued before the Israelites and did not raise its head again. During Gideon's lifetime, the land enjoyed peace forty years. Judges 8:28

TABLE TALK

1. What do you pray will be your legacy?

2. What will you do as a man and as a Squad to expand the presence of the King on earth?

THE VISION OF THE PHALANX

"I was wearing the full armor of God, riding alone on a journey to a faraway, darkened land. Like a Don Quixote, I saw in the distance my destination…an ominous fortress of stone that grew larger as I approached. Walls of slate grey rose fifty feet tall and twenty feet thick, surrounding the Keep. Bronze gates as high reinforced with iron, were closed at my path.

This was the place I knew God had called me to go…and, forgetting the Mighty King whom I served, I trembled inside.

Then, as if brought to me by the wind, rising from the dungeons below, I heard the groans of men from my homeland…and the haunting rattle of chains. I could almost feel the yearning of their hearts for freedom, and I felt too their despair of ever being rescued.

Bent upon doing something for my countrymen, I spurred my charger down the hardened pathway that led to the massive gates of the castle. Reigning in as I approached, I dismounted and hastened to the portcullis. With a newfound determination, I began leveling blows upon the gates with my shield and sword, commanding them to yield in the Name of the King, and I cried out to anyone who might hear inside the walls, to set my brethren free!

For a short while, nothing happened…and then, from up above, I heard a voice on the upper wall to my left, "Halloo man-child, it is only the fool who comes to these gates alone, and expects to live." Several others joined in with jeers and heckling laughter. "He's mine," snarled one of my mockers…"No, mine," barked another.

The next thing I heard was the thwang! of a bow. The sound was immediately followed by an arrow, tipped in pitch and aflame, which struck the ground near my boot. It was followed by another, and I raised my shield just in time to quench several more as they began to find their mark. I was pinned to the ground…alone in my zeal and foolishness. At that moment, I began to fear…and offered a desperate prayer for deliverance.

It was then that I first heard the sound of a distant horn. Not the brazen blast of the enemy, but the pure, beautiful wind of the horn of Gideon…the horn that only could come from my country. The rain of arrows ceased and I then heard the mustering to arms from within the gates.

Looking to the source of the horn, I gazed over the hillside to see the rise of scores…no, hundreds, of armed men. As some of the men came into focus, I could see fierceness in their countenance; hard faces, set like flints. Then I heard the horn sound a second time and a troop of foot soldiers arranged in a formation that looked like a living spear came charging down the path that I had just taken. A battle cry rose from their throats and it was mixed with the anthem song of praises to our King.

They had formed a phalanx of about a score of men in each of three rows; two rows on the outside and another in between. The center column was wielding a large armored battering ram. Sixty men moving with a single purpose. I had seen this ram before and remembered that on the one side of the ram were carved the words "THE PRAYERS OF THE SAINTS," and on the other, "THE VENGEANCE OF OUR LORD."

I saw some of the men raise their shields over the men carrying the ram and others lifting theirs, interlocked now, on both sides. Continuing their advance, the beautiful canopy, a mosaic of red with the crest of the Lion of the Judah, was complete.

In moments, it seemed, the men were over me, covering me so I might rise with them and, then together, with the Name of our King on our lips, we assaulted the gate. The booming sound was deafening, and the ground shook. We rained blow after blow. Some began to tire with me, but we continued on. Then on the what must have been the hundredth blow, there was an impossible shuddering…a high pitched screech of metal tearing away from metal, and the gates began to give way…"

An excerpt from "Called to War: Out of the Stands…Into the Arena," by Art Hobba

CORE CONDITIONING

- *CORE Offering*

NOTE: This Warrior course was in part, brought to you by the foresight and generosity of other brothers in Christ. Thank you for making it possible that others may step into the arena as well.

ARMOR OF GOD CONVEYANCE

- *Conveyance is as follows:*

  a. Form a short (2-3 leaders) reception line in he front of the room. The lead teacher should be at the front of he line and maybe the men's leader, room Captain or pastor in the 2nd position. The second or third man can keep fresh coins coming to he lead man.

  b. Have each Squad Leader bring his able, one table at a time, to form a line on the right of the Leader (Stage Left)

  c. Hold the coin in the palm of your hand, palm facing upwards, and reach out to the Warrior receiving his coin with a handshake motion. He reaches as well and places his hand on top of your hand.

  d. As you shake his hand, rotate you wrist counterclockwise so the coin falls into his hand by gravity.

  e. Holding his hand and drawing him towards you, speak the words into his heart "Walk worthy!" He then responds, "So others may live!"

  f. Embrace the man and let him move down towards the right he reception line where he is charged and embraced in he same way. He then returns with his Squad to his table.

ARMOR UP!

1. By faith, I gird my core up with Truth

2. By faith, I put on the Shoes as an Ambassador of the good news of Your Kingdom

3. By faith, and because I am forgiven and holy before You, I put on the Breastplates of Righteousness

4. By faith, because I have been given Your spiritual mind, I put on the Helmet of Salvation

5. Then Lord, I take up the shield of Your faithfulness and the Sword of Your living, powerful Spirit.

I am more than a Conqueror. Thank You Jesus for the Victory!

WHAT'S NEXT?

1. **No man left behind:** In America the church's reaction to someone falling away of falling or even on their sword has to often been less than loving. Be alert…and love them enough to rescue the wounded (and sometimes even the stupid).

2. **Expect engagement from Satan and his cohorts.** You are much more ready that before but god will allow you to be tested in your armor, so put it on every morning.

3. **Maintain your 911** by calling them <u>at least once per week</u> and meeting twice month

4. **Practice and only settle for authenticity.** Only trust a man who will show you his scars!

5. **DEPLOYMENT: Serve in the arena with your Squad!** Ask God to help you find a need in your church or community or neighborhood and join with fellow squad members to give yourself away, asking God to help you gain ground for the advance of his Kingdom and be a bringer of righteousness, joy and peace in Jesus Name.

6. **Gather again soon to experience the next stage of Core 300 discipleship.** Recruit new men to the Warrior and then enter "The Priest", the second in the excitin three part Core 300 series.

FOUNDER

Art Hobba blends twenty-five years of experience in business, founding **Transcende** (www.trancende.net), a corporate coaching and consulting firm, with two decades of senior pastoral and men's ministry leadership. In 2008 he founded **Core 300** (www.core300.org) where he serves the Body of Christ by calling men "out of the stands" of shame and mediocrity, and into the arena of their destiny.

Art lives in Agoura Hills, California, with his wife Sharon, and enjoys writing, skiing and everything about the sea; including spearfishing and diving. His five sons still visit often enough to enjoy regular "refrigerator rights."

You can contact Art for speaking engagements, retreats, and consulting or organizational team building at our website.

The Core 300™ Series

Book 1: Called to War: *Out of the Stands...Into the Arena!*

Book 2: The Battle-Priest: *Bowed in Surrender...Swept up into Victory!* (available in 2011)

Book 3: The Shepherd-King: *Bound in Service...Crowned into Dominion!* (available in 2012)

Contact Us
Core 300
PO Box 1202
Agoura Hills, CA. 91301-1202
Phone: (877) 606-4609

Join us! at FaceBook Core 300

Visit our website:
http://www.core300.org/WarriorLaunch.htm
Warrior Launch Kit: ISBN 978-0-9845101-8-4

ENLIST IN THE CORE 300 RESERVES!

YES! I want to "*Pay it Forward*" by becoming a member of the
Core 300 Reserves :

___ Please add me to the **Core 300 SWAT Team** to pray each day for Core 300

Monthly Donation Amount (please check the appropriate box)

$10 [ ] $25 [ ] $40 [ ] $50 [ ] $100 [ ] $500 [ ] $1000 [ ]

Billing Frequency   [ ] Monthly

                              [ ] Quarterly

Other $_____ (one-time donation)

___

E-mail _____

Phone (_____) _____

Name on Card or Check_____

Billing Address _____ City, _____State, _____Zip____

Card No: | | | | | | | | | | | | | | | | | | | |

Expires _____ / _____ (XX/XXXX)

Authentication Code _____3 digits (MC/VISA/DISC) or 4 digits (AMEX) on back of card

Cash/Check [Check #_____]

Signature _____

Please Tear out and Fax (866.280.7092} or Mail to:

Core 300, P.O. Box 1202, Agoura Hills, CA 91301-1202